AN ORGANIC APPROACH TO STRUCTURING YOUR BOOK

AN ORGANIC APPROACH TO STRUCTURING YOUR BOOK

A Right-Brained Alternative to Outlines (Workbook Included)

NAOMI ROSE

Rose Press

An Organic Approach to Structuring Your Book: A Right-Brained Alternative to Outlines (Workbook Included), by Naomi Rose. Copyright © 2023 by Naomi Rose. All rights reserved.

Published by Rose Press
www.rosepress.com
rosepressbooks@yahoo.com

This book may not be reproduced in whole or in part, in any form or by any means, electronic or mechanical, including recording, or by any information storage and retrieval system now known or hereafter invented, without written permission of the publisher. Brief excerpts may be quoted, in print or online, for the purpose of book reviews and articles about the book.

However, purchasers of this book are free to print out or otherwise copy the workbook "Reflections" pages for their own use.

Interior book design: Naomi Rose.

Illustrations: Naomi Rose. Copyright © 2023 by Naomi Rose. All rights reserved.

The material in this book is based on the "Writing from the Deeper Self" approach to book development created by Naomi Rose, as put forth on her website: www.naomirose.net

First edition. Published 2023.
Printed in the United States of America.
ISBN #: 978-0-9983928-4-4

Contents

WELCOME TO THIS BOOK AND YOUR EVOLVING TABLE OF CONTENTS   1

One
A BOOK (IDEA) IS BORN!   5

Two
HOW EVOLVING A TABLE OF CONTENTS DIFFERS FROM STARTING WITH AN OUTLINE   18

Three
HOW TO EVOLVE A TABLE OF CONTENTS   36

Four
AN ILLUSTRATION OF THE PROCESS   74

APPENDIX   93
NEXT STEPS . . .   99
ABOUT NAOMI ROSE   103
ROSE PRESS: A PUBLISHING HOUSE FOR YOUR INNER GARDEN   107
OTHER BOOKS & ART BY NAOMI ROSE   111

List of Workbook Reflections

Chapter One: A Book (Idea) Is Born!
Reflection 1: Your Experience with Outlines 11
Reflection 2: Are You More Top-Down, Bottom-Up, or Somewhere in Between? 14

Chapter Two: How Evolving a Table of Contents Differs from Starting with an Outline
Reflection 3: Re-Trace Your Path of Inspiration 28
Reflection 4: What "More" of You Hasn't Yet Been Invited into Your Writing? 33

Chapter Three: How to Evolve a Table of Contents
Reflection 5: Accessing Your Heart's Wisdom through Its Rhythm 41
Reflection 6: Enlist Your Body to Help Evolve Your TOC 44
Reflection 7: Steeping 47
Reflection 8: Incubating a Response During Sleep 51
Reflection 9: Meditating on Your TOC 56
Reflection 10: Praying About What Belongs in Your Book 60
Reflection 11: Integrating Your Glimmers into a More Whole Picture 64
Reflection 12: Giving the Cognitive Mind Its Right Place in Structuring
Your Book 69

Chapter Four: An Illustration of the Process
Reflection 13: Clarifying What You Have Learned 86

List of Illustrations

Chapter One: A Book (Idea!) Is Born
A Book (Idea!) Is Born 6
Young Man Writing an Outline 9

Chapter Two: How Evolving a Table of Contents Differs from Starting with an Outline
How Evolving a Table of Contents Differs from Starting with an Outline 19
Your TOC *Looks* Like an Outline, but It Comes from the Other Direction 21
A Castle in the Air 25
A Sculpture Made of Clay 26

Chapter Three: How to Evolve a Table of Contents
How to Evolve a Table of Contents 37
The Rhythmic Heart 40
Body Intelligence (What Does Your Body Have to Tell You?) 43
Steeping Inspirations for Your TOC 46
Sleeping on Your Inspirations 50
Woman Sitting in Meditation 55
Man in Prayer 58
Reaching for the Glimmerings 63

Chapter Four: An Illustration of the Process
An Illustration of the Process 75
A Look Back at the TOC Process (from Glimmerings to an Evolving TOC) 83

And assorted leaves and flowers in various stages of growth.

ACKNOWLEDGMENTS

My first acknowledgment needs to go to the larger book I was in the process of writing, *Growing Your Book by Listening to What's Inside You: A Writing from the Deeper Self Approach*, out of which the idea for this book-with-workbook came. Only a single chapter in that book addressed the subject of writing without an outline (based on my own way of putting that book together), but once written down it became clear to me that a good deal more on the subject could be explored and written. Following that call led to the book you are reading now, which pleases me no end. So I thank not only the book, but the creative process itself, which seeds possibilities in our consciousness and then gives us the means to follow them and see where they go. This has been a rich and fruitful journey.

As for the human support and feedback I received, I want especially to thank the following people:

My husband, Ralph Dranow--writer, editor, poet, and master of succinctness. I always know that his feedback on my writing will be truthful and caring, and that any overdone floweriness on my part will receive the benefit of his adept pruning. In the case of this book, his pruning shears were dormant 99 percent of the time. His eyes lit up as he gave the printout back to me, and he said the lovely things about the book that now appear on its back cover.

My good friend Dana Watt, spiritual co-traveler, creative being, and the only person I know who has an inherent gift for marketing (she reads marketing books for pleasure) and sees it as spiritual service. I turned to her when the first draft of this book was barely done, and the many wonderful, life-giving suggestions she provided were so clearly valuable that I took almost all of them. (You have her to thank for the pull quotes, Appendix, and a great deal more.) This wouldn't be the book it is without her input.

And my good friend Jane Majkiewicz, a writer, editor, lover of literacy, and generous creative soul whose feedback is always ample, considered, and beyond encouraging. To have Jane to turn to before loosing my writings to the world provides earth beneath my feet, wind under my wings, and more ingenious ideas for ways to put forth the book than would ever occur to me on my own.

Thanks to the support of these beloved friends, I can honestly say that this book might change your life if there's a book you've wanted to write but didn't want to subject yourself to writing an outline. Now, you don't have to.

*This book is for those who aren't fond of a top-down approach to outlining,
and wish there were a way to get their book on track
that better fits their writing style.*

*And it's also for those who do tend towards a top-down approach,
but wish they could tap the innate creativity
they may not yet fully know they have.*

To all the wonderful would-be book writers
with something valuable to say
and a beautiful soul from which to say it
who have struggled with outlines (or the prospect of writing one)
and either written an outline-based book that worked okay but didn't sing
or let go of writing the book, and felt discouraged about it and themselves -

*There was never anything wrong with you.
You just had a different way of creating.*

May this book and workbook speak to your own intrinsic ways and being
so you can write the book of your heart and love the process,
including evolving a Table of Contents

A NOTE ON WORKING WITH THE WORKBOOK

This book includes integrated Workbook sections called "Reflections."

During your times of reflection on what's addressed in this book,
you can write in the Workbook pages directly.
Or you can refer to them while writing in a separate notebook or journal.

Either way (or both), may your Reflections connect you to the place within
that wants to write and structure a book without requiring an outline.
(It absolutely can be done! Read on. . . .)

WELCOME TO THIS BOOK AND YOUR EVOLVING TABLE OF CONTENTS

In my decades-long work as a Book Developer and Creative Midwife helping people write the book of their heart, I've noticed how many of them struggle with the structure of their book — try to shoehorn their sometimes messy inspirations into an outline (or can't *find* any inspiration) — then either buckle down to fill it in, or just can't make themselves do that and feel they're failing their book and themselves.

But there's a big difference between coming up with an outline before writing your book, and *evolving a Table of Contents* (TOC) as you go.

This book will introduce you to the process of evolving a TOC, show you what it might look like, and enable you to experience for yourself how it can open up your creative/connective intelligence as well as making good use of your logical intelligence so you can bring all of yourself to writing your book and even be nourished by the process.

First, I'll explain what it means to evolve a TOC and why it's beneficial.

Then I'll show you how it works.

Finally, I'll give an illustration I came up with using the same Writing from the Deeper Self process that I lay out and that you'll be making use of. Along the way, you'll have the opportunity to play with your own process so you can find the arc of your book organically, in a way that fits you, reflects you, and even inspires you.

I recommend that after you've read through this book, you read it again — perhaps more than once! — with a pen or pencil (and maybe a notebook) by your side. This will give you more time and space in which to record your "glimmers" (explanation to come), questions, responses, and written expressions in the "Reflections" sections of the workbook part. This habit will spark you into organically evolving a Table of Contents that invites the book of your heart to reveal itself so you can write it.

~ Naomi Rose,
Book Developer & Creative Midwife
Creator, Writing from the Deeper Self
www.naomirose.net

A TABLE OF CONTENTS CAN BE WRITTEN OUT OF ORDER AND LATER PUT INTO A SEQUENCE THAT LOOKS DESIGNED THAT WAY FROM THE START.

One

A BOOK (IDEA) IS BORN!

CHAPTER ONE — A BOOK IDEA IS BORN!

NOTE: This chapter offers the following Workbook "Reflections" to help you find your way conceptually and concretely:

- Reflection 1: "Your Experience with Outlines"
- Reflection 2: "Are You More Top-Down, Bottom-Up, or Somewhere in Between?"

> *The real difference between starting with an outline and evolving a Table of Contents isn't in what the ingredients look like when they're done. It's in how they get there in the first place.*

Congratulations! You've decided to write a book! This is the start of an important journey, one that wouldn't even begin unless the desire to write a book was in you. Your decision to write a book is a sign that you believe you have something significant to say and to offer readers — something that will help them, inspire them, educate them, or in some other way benefit them. It also suggests that something has called you to do it.

Maybe you have always wanted to write a book. Maybe you already consider yourself a writer at heart and are ready to go bigger with a book-length offering. Perhaps your motivation is to make an impact on the world . . . or use your book to build or further strengthen your career . . . or something else. Or maybe you *never* thought of writing a book before, but now it has visited your thoughts and doesn't want to leave.

So the desire is all-important, and you have already internally experienced it. Being called from within to write a book, and saying "Yes!" (as you have) will see you through.

Still, you may not yet have much of a sense of what the road ahead will look like, or where to place your feet on the path. Typically, writers of nonfiction books (including but not limited to first-time authors) will look around for some formula to get them started and keep them going. And there are many formulas available! "Write a book in a weekend!" "Come up with an outline, and then just fill it in!" The outline-based approach is a standard prescription, often starting as far back as middle school and extending into graduate school and PhD dissertations. So for those who have been exposed to this approach over the years, it might seem like a no-brainer.

But it doesn't fit for everyone. It requires a certain way of thinking, and pretty much *only* that way of thinking. And what if you just aren't put together that way — what then? Must you shoehorn yourself and your book-to-be into a convention that fails to inspire you? That makes you feel you have to hunker down and produce something that doesn't organically come from within you? That doesn't reflect the *real* you? And why would you even want to spend time and energy to write a book that didn't?

The fact that many nonfiction books tend to follow a generic format *and* get published doesn't mean this is the best, or the only, way to write a book. Much better, in my view, is to write a book that's *alive* for you as you write it . . . that brings forth *more* of you, so you end up even richer and more self-actualized than before . . . that makes use of your uniquely creative nature (even if you aren't yet fully aware of what it is or how it works for you).

Starting with an outline or some other prescriptive formula may get the job done. But this may sacrifice an intimate, fresh, full-of-discovery relationship with your book, as it gradually shows itself to you. Besides, to tell yourself ahead of time what your book will be about from A to Z can eclipse the light of the creative process that's inherent in you as well as your book.

It's understandable that you might want to seek out a formula and follow it, especially if you haven't written a book before. The unknowns of writing a book can seem overwhelming, at first: "What do I do? Where do I start? How do I know I even have it in me to do it?"

As someone who was trained *out of* my innate creativity by much of my schooling, and then by the industry standards of my profession for the first several decades of my adult life (I was a book editor working for publishers), I know how having a formula to follow — even a relative formula — can provide a sense of confidence about being on track. When I wrote magazine articles for publication, I started with an outline. When I saw my byline at the end of the printed magazine, I felt a rush of pride: *"I did that!"* But over time, I knew that who I *was*, inside, was nowhere to be seen. And after a while, this absence of authenticity—of soul, you could say—began to weigh on me, and the byline in print was not worth its price.

I believe it's entirely possible to write a terrific book—one that interests its readers and does well for its publishers—*and* be true to yourself in the writing. And one way to go about this is to forego the outlines, forego thinking you need to know exactly what you're going to do at the outset, and offer your wider span of intelligences (not only the cognitive intelligence responsible for architecting an outline) the opportunity to offer their gifts.

And that's what this book (workbook included) will give you access to: a more organic, right-brained way to structure the book that's in you to write. Along the way, you may encounter inner capacities that you didn't even know were there. So many possibilities lie ahead of you, not only for your book but also for your understanding of who you are.

DOES AN OUTLINE *HAVE* TO BE THE FIRST STEP?

So here you are, ready to write a book. What comes to mind to do first?

Most of us have been taught to start by coming up with an outline, so you know what you're going to say before you say it. Point #1, point #2, point #3, and so on all the way to the Conclusion. Then it's a simple matter of just filling all those items in:

- Point 1: _____
- Point 2: _____
- Point 3: _____ (and so on).

Well . . . not necessarily.

For one thing, not everyone is intrinsically good at outlines. And even those who are good at lists and logical progression still can hit a blank wall once they are faced with a string of points to address. Because naming the ideas is one thing, but bringing them to life with details that are engaging and meaningful for others to read (and for you to write!) is another.

And yet the unexamined belief is that you *have* to start with an outline. Otherwise, the fear is that you'll be all over the place with your writing, and won't really be able to progress.

> *Naming the ideas is one thing, but bringing them to life with details that are engaging and meaningful for others to read (and for you to write!) is another.*

WE ARE CONDITIONED TO THINK IN TERMS OF OUTLINES

Many of us have come away from our schooling with the conviction that we *must* begin a work of writing with an outline — especially in the case of nonfiction, where the creative process may be considered (if it even *is* considered) irrelevant.

And it's not just schooling. Starting with an outline is still the prevalent view, especially for producing a book. There are numerous webinars and expensive courses on outline writing that promise smooth sailing for the actual writing of the book once this element is in place. "Just come up with a solid outline," they declare, "and your book will write itself. Here's how to do it." As if having a mental construction of a sequence to be filled in were all there is to it, something that anyone can learn to do.

Well, maybe anyone *can* learn to follow a formula (though I'm not so sure about that), but at what cost? What gets left out of the *person* doing the writing that could more inclusively be invited in?

You can reflect on this for yourself in the following Workbook Reflection, "Your Experience with Outlines."

~ WORKBOOK ~

REFLECTION 1
Your Experience with Outlines

What were you taught about coming up with an outline for your writing?

Have you actually used outlines when you wrote (e.g., in school / for your career — blogs / articles /etc.)?

YES: _____   NO: _____

If you *did* use outlines:

- Can you recall what it was like for you to devise them?
- Did they help you write what you set out to write?
- Did you feel freed-up during the writing process, or like you were mostly filling in the blanks, or what?
- Did you emerge from the writing-according-to-the-outline with a sense of discovery, refreshment, pleasure at the capacities you got to use, even delight? Or something else?

If you did *not* use outlines:

- Did you feel overwhelmed by the ideas that swirled in your mind, and not know how to get them down so that they fully made sense?

- Did you feel faced with a stockpile of details without having a way to organize and contain them?

- Did you procrastinate writing your project until the last moment because it seemed so confusing as to what to do?

- Did you find some gems in the writing as you went along, ideas and phrasing that surprised you with your capabilities, but still felt the writing didn't hang together as a whole?

- Were you rewarded for your effort *internally*? Or did you come out of the experience feeling deficient in some way?

{This Reflection practice now comes to a close. You can continue in a notebook, now or later, if you like.}

Who Outlines Do and Don't Work For

The Top-Down Approach: The logical, top-down approach involved in outlining works for people who *already* lead with a logical, top-down approach in their lives. People who think like engineers, scientists, tech specialists, and others who see through a predominantly mental, left-brained lens — even musicians and others who are known for their technique. Of course, we *all* have a logical left-brained aspect of our being, and we need it to give structure and organization to our observations and experiences. But there are situations — including writing a nonfiction book — where it may not always be most helpful to *lead* with it.

But even for the logically minded, an outline has certain limitations: for one thing, just because you've written one doesn't mean it tells you how to actually fill it in. As they say, the map is not the territory. Just because you've come up with a map to follow ("Write about Point A, then write about Point B, then Point C") doesn't mean you know *how* to say what you've set yourself up to say. The "territory" of writing is not always linear, and strictly linear writing is rarely engaging.

> *The logical, top-down approach involved in outlining works for people who already lead with a logical, top-down approach in their lives. Just because you've written an outline doesn't mean it tells you how to actually fill it in.*

The Bottom-Up Approach: And for people who are more at home with the "bottom-up" approach of starting with the details and feeling their way through them to some kind of conclusion via non-logical leaps of connection — a predominantly right-brained lens — starting with an outline can feel more of an imposition than a help, distancing their creative mind/heart from the very source of creation they rely on.

Because once the outline is written, what do you do then? Filling it in isn't always as simple as coloring within the boundary lines that have been drawn. Without inspiration, without a felt connection to the material, what gets written can lie there lifeless on the page, doing its job of relating to the outline but failing to make full use of the writer's rich inner being (whether known to the writer or not), and so coming out sounding generic, flat, interchangeable with other writings on the same topic that someone else could have written.

It may get the job done, on a certain level, but not in a way that's truly satisfying to the writer — or to the reader.

You can reflect on this for yourself in the following Workbook Reflection, "Are You More Top-Down, Bottom-Up, or Somewhere in Between?"

~ WORKBOOK ~

REFLECTION 2
Are You More Top-Down, Bottom-Up, or Somewhere in Between?

Where do you see yourself on the spectrum of top-down/left brain and bottom-up/right brain? We all have both, but perhaps we are more naturally dominant in one area than the other. Or it might vary depending on the circumstances.

For example, as an artist I'm pretty left-brained about my tools — choosing them, using them for their intended purpose, caring for them so they last and function optimally. But then when I'm actually *using* these tools, my right-brained intelligence is in the forefront, making connections on a nonverbal level that affect the composition, the balance of form and space, and even that take me out of linear time so that passing hours feel like minutes. My joy occurs in that connecting, but thinking through my tools supports my letting go into nonverbal experience. So on a scale from 1 to 10 (itself a left-brain categorization), with 1 being totally left-brained and 10 being totally right-brained, with my tools I'm at around 2, and with the actual art-making I'm at 10.

Reflect on three different activities you have experienced that called on your capacities in some way. Maybe you wrote a blog, or cooked a meal, or gave a speech, for example. Where on the spectrum would you place yourself in terms of "top-down/left brain" and "bottom-up/right brain" for each of the three activities (where "1" is "extremely left-brain," "5" is "both brains," and "10" is "extremely right-brain"?

1 _____ 5 _____ 10

Extremely left-brain   **Both**   **Extremely right-brain**

Activity #1:

What it was: _____

Where you'd place it on the spectrum: _____

Activity #2:

What it was: _____

Where you'd place it on the spectrum: _____

Activity #3:

What it was: _____

Where you'd place it on the spectrum: _____

Your Assessment:

Were the numbers that you assigned to each of these activities close to one another, or distant?
_____

What might this suggest to you about how you tend to approach activities on the spectrum of left-brain and/or right-brain?

Do you feel satisfied and complete with this way? If so, what about it is satisfying?

If you do *not* feel satisfied with this way, what about it is unsatisfying?

Could you envision a potential benefit in exploring the less-developed way — that is, bottom-up if you tend towards top-down, and top-down if you tend towards bottom-up? If so, what activity comes to mind that you might try? (If nothing comes to you right now, don't worry. You'll have an opportunity to use *both* approaches later on in this book.)

How might your understanding of your dominant approach affect how you go about determining what goes into your book (i.e., coming up with an outline or evolving a TOC)?

{This Reflection practice now comes to a close. You can continue in a notebook, now or later, if you like.}

While probably anyone *can* learn to write an outline, it isn't always the best fit for a given writer, and so it's important to realize that there is an alternative. (There's probably more than one alternative, but this is what I've come up with based on my work with book-writing clients as well as my own experience). And that is to *evolve a Table of Contents*. The notion that this process *evolves* is liberating, and frees you from a formulaic approach that ultimately might not feel right for you.

Two

HOW EVOLVING A TABLE OF CONTENTS DIFFERS FROM STARTING WITH AN OUTLINE

CHAPTER TWO

DIFFERS FROM STARTING WITH AN OUTLINE · HOW EVOLVING A TABLE OF CONTENTS

NOTE: This chapter offers the following Workbook "Reflections" to help you find your way conceptually and concretely:

- Reflection 3: "Re-Trace Your Path of Inspiration"
- Reflection 4: "What 'More' of You Hasn't Yet Been Invited into Your Writing?"

At first glance, a Table of Contents (TOC) appears to be nearly identical to a book outline. They both list the parts, the chapters, and sometimes even the main headings in developmental order: first Chapter 1 about X, then Chapter 2 about Y, then Chapter 3 about Z, and so on.

True, the Table of Contents shows up towards the beginning of a published book, whereas an outline is just for the writer, constructed for the purpose of writing the manuscript. But the real difference isn't in what the ingredients look like when they're done. It's in how they get there in the first place.

In an **outline**, you start your book writing by coming up at the outset with a logical, developmental order detailing what's going to be covered in the book, in what sequence, and what the hierarchy will be (which subsections will be part of which larger sections). So first you figure out what will be in Chapter 1, then you figure out what will be in Chapter 2, then Chapter 3, and so on until the end. Then you fill in each of these categories with writing.

But in this Deeper Self approach to developing a **Table of Contents** for your manuscript,[2] you start by actually *writing* something — something that gives itself to you, resonates with you, interests you.

That is, you let your creative right-brain lead where it leads.

Then you back up, bring in your logical, categorizing mind, and see what you've just written is all about.

Now you have the beginning of a topic that's based on actual writing. You won't have to push yourself to fill in the blanks. You can simply give a name to what you already have written.

> *In developing a Table of Contents for your manuscript, you start by actually writing something that gives itself to you, that resonates with you. You let your creative right-brain lead. Then you back up, bring in your logical, categorizing mind, and see what you've just written is all about. Now you have the beginnings of a topic that's based on actual writing. You won't have to push yourself to fill in the blanks.*

This is the essence of what evolving a Table of Contents is about. The rest of this book will give you the details.

~~~~~~~~~

[2] Your manuscript is your writing as it progresses, before it becomes an actual book.

Your TOC Looks Like an Outline, but It Comes from the Other Direction

As it's filled in over time, your Table of Contents gradually comes to look a lot like an outline. The difference is that you don't *write* it from the top down in sequential order, and then have to figure out how to fill it in. Instead, you write *whatever gives itself to you, in the order that gives itself to you.*

This is really important. When you write what calls to you in the moment, at least two deeply wonderful things happen:

One, there's no resistance, no having to make yourself do it. You're already writing as you are called to.

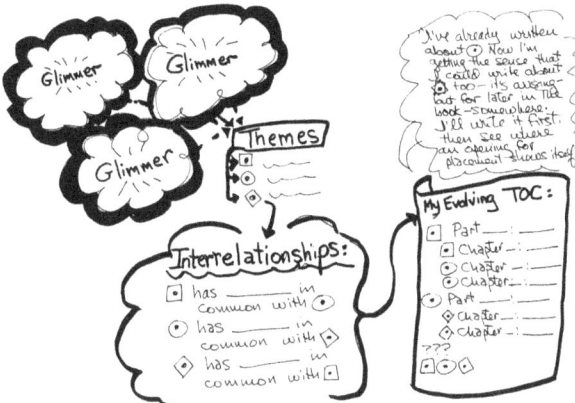

Two, in following this "what calls me?" route, you have an excellent chance of making contact with the Source of inspiration — the guidance that called you to write a book in the first place — as it wants to come through you. Call it "intuition," call it "my Divine connection" — whatever you call it, it's here for you if you turn towards it.

> *You have an excellent chance of making contact with the Source of inspiration — the guidance that called you to write a book in the first place — as it wants to come through you. Call it "intuition," call it "my Divine connection" — whatever you call it, it's here for you if you turn towards it.*

Finding What Else Your Writing-Piece Relates to: Of course, you might object that this is all well and good, but what if you end up with a pile of disconnected writings? The "Writing from the Deeper Self" approach has this covered, too. You don't just write something, stockpile it, and write something else. After you write something, then you back up to see that piece *in relation* to the other pieces, so you can begin to sense where what you've written belongs in the larger scheme of your book. Even if you don't yet *have* a larger scheme for your book, the accumulation of pieces of living writing[3] will begin to show the larger territory over time.

~~~~~~~~~~

[3] I call writing that has given itself to you "living writing," in contrast to the kind of *labored* writing that often comes from a top-down approach. Living writing gives you something that interests, often even nourishes you when you read what you have written.

The Sequencing Happens Along the Way: Eventually, your TOC will appear on the page with its parts listed in sequential order. But *the sequencing happens along the way, as the writing unfolds*, not at the beginning. In the beginning, you might have, somewhere on your TOC, a title for the first piece you wrote and then—mostly as a placeholder, not necessarily meant to immediately follow the first piece—the title of a second piece.

> *Eventually, your TOC will appear on the page with its parts listed in sequential order. But the sequencing happens along the way, as the writing unfolds, not at the beginning.*

An example of an early TOC follows. The sections in bold are written; placing them in the TOC anchors an indication of the evolving structure. (Some sketchy thoughts are added in brackets to indicate my process.)

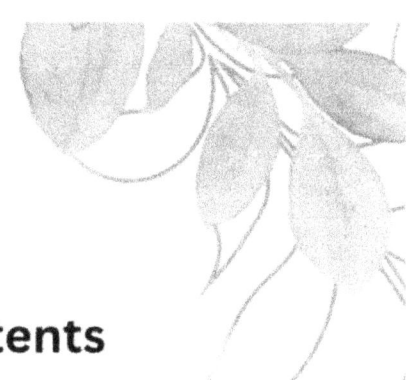

Table of Contents

We Are Conditioned to Think in Terms of Outlines
[Will this be a part, a chapter, or a main heading? It seems pretty central.]

[Chapter to come]

[Chapter to come]

[Chapter to come]

Steeping
[An important detail that really speaks to what I'm seeking to say. It just gave itself to me, and I like how it came out. Maybe it could be part of a larger section on creative intelligence?]

[Chapter to come]

[Chapter to come....]

Only later, once you glean a sense of the form and structure that's inherent in the pieces (the whole that the pieces slowly start to suggest), do you start to put the pieces into a sequence that looks like a deliberate Table of Contents. In the above example, these scant two insertions — "We Are Conditioned to Think in Terms of Outlines" and "Steeping"[4] — are enough to begin to show an evolving sense of the shape of the book. They don't indicate everything, but what's there is substantial because it's already been written.

The Path Begins to Reveal Itself

At some point, enough traction has been created by what you've written and entered into the Table of Contents so far that you can see where the developmental arc is *naturally* going. This shines a trustworthy light on your path. From that point on, what you write can go with that direction for as long as it feels organically true. (And if, down the road, what you wrote shifts the direction of the book, by that time you'll be used to this dynamic movement and able to flow with it until your book truly settles in and tells you, "This is what I am.") It's an interactive process, not a prescriptive one:

- You invite the writing to come to you.
- You welcome it and write it down when it does.
- You give it a working title that speaks to what that piece of writing is about.
- You place it in your TOC where it intuitively seems to belong.
- Later, you may realize that a different order works better, or that you need to write a new section to follow up on what's in the TOC.
- So you invite the writing to come to you.
- And so on.

This allows inspiration and interest to be your guide rather than forcing on yourself a dutiful and uninspired outlined list. You can see that it's a creative process, even at this early point. As you follow your intuition, you find your originality and writing "voice."

> *At some point, enough traction has been created by what you've written and entered into the Table of Contents so far that you can see where the developmental arc is naturally going.*

~~~~~~~~~~

[4] You'll get to read about "Steeping" in Chapter Three.

Plus, creativity is good for you. It intrinsically *feels* good. Inspiration gives you more breath (inspire = to breathe). The spacious calm that you may sense in yourself at such moments not only brings unexpected treasures to the surface to be written but also soothes your nervous system, stimulating higher reaches of the brain and deeper reaches of the heart.

A DIFFERENT, MORE RECEPTIVE MODEL
A CASTLE IN THE AIR / A STATUE MADE OF CLAY, NOT STONE

Metaphors to do with writing often use a different model than this approach to evolving a TOC — like building a house from the ground up, or making a sculpture in stone.

Building a House

The Erecting-a-House-from-the-Foundation-Up Model: This deeper approach to evolving a Table of Contents is *not*, for example, like building a house brick by brick, where the foundation must be dug and laid before the ground-floor scaffolding can be erected on top of it — the flooring, walls, windows, doors, ceiling, chimney, and roof, in that order. In the actual building of a house, that order *must* be followed. You can't start with the roof and work your way down to the ground.

The Castle-in-the-Air Model: But you *can* (metaphorically) start with the roof in this approach you're discovering here. Evolving your Table of Contents is more like building a "castle in the air." You allow the creative process to lead you. Of course, it *ends up* as a tangible manifestation ("the house"), but it doesn't *begin* in that realm. The call that you receive to write a book, the inspiration — however insistent — is wispier than that at first, more subtle, more unformed. Eventually, it will work its way down to the foundation, but it's not at that solid state yet.

But this is the way of inspiration.

As Henry David Thoreau put it, "If you have built castles in the air, your work need not be lost; that is where they should be. Now put foundations under them." Evolving a Table of Contents instead of starting with an outline is in line with this honored tradition.

> *Evolving your Table of Contents is more like building a "castle in the air." You allow the creative process to lead you. There's a discovery to be had, more unearthing than implementing.*

I don't mean to disparage the metaphor of comparing writing to building a house from the foundation up. You *can* do it this way, and many have done it. There is much to recommend this approach, in certain cases. But not everyone operates this way, intrinsically; and the point of Writing from the Deeper Self is to find the way that fits for *you*. This inspiration-first approach is how the Kabbalistic Tree of Life presents the process of manifestation: First comes the inspiration. Eventually, it works its way through the less dense spheres to more and more solid spheres, until is made evident, solid, and real.

Making a Sculpture

The Sculpting-in-Stone Model: Evolving a TOC is also unlike carving a sculpture in stone. There, having a plan before you even pick up your chisel is paramount, because you can take bits of stone *away* from the larger block in the process of moving towards the creation of a deliberate form, but you can't then change your mind and put the bits of stone that have been removed *back*. (You *can* change direction in response and work with what's left of the stone, but that's often experienced as making the best of an error.)

The Sculpting-with-Clay Model: If writing a book from the Deeper Self by evolving a Table of Contents were a sculpture, it wouldn't be set in stone. It would be molded from a pliable substance like clay — moist and malleable, connecting more directly with its maker hand-to-clay than a distancing chisel allows for — a handful-after-handful communication between the body of the maker and the body of what's being made.

This is a way of sculpting that offers latitude not only for correcting "mistakes" (it's easy enough to scoop off bits that don't sit well, or to add bits of clay and smooth them in to extend the emerging form) but also for working *with* the emergent properties of the creation, giving it room to let the sculptor sense what it wants to become. And a sculpture in clay can be kept moist for the entire length of its creation.

Only once the sculptor has declared the piece complete is it left to dry and harden to the point where it can no longer be worked on. This is like signing "The End" at the completion of a manuscript, and meaning it.

> *Sculpting in clay rather than stone is a malleable, handful-after-handful communication between the body of the maker and the body of what's being made.*

You see where I'm going with this. If you're writing the kind of book that's enough like a house that you can say, "Okay, foundation dug — check. Floorboards installed — check. Wall scaffolding — check. Drywall — check," and so on, then an outline will do you fine. But if there's a discovery to be had, more unearthing than implementing, well, then you need something more on the order of a castle in the air revealing itself — and only gradually reaching down for its foundation.

With an outline-based approach, the foundation is a given. But with the evolving-a-Table-of-Contents approach, the foundation may show up along the way as something of a surprise: "Oh, I hadn't realized I was writing a book about ____, but what do you know, I am!" When this happens, it can be cause for celebration rather than panic. It means there's an *aliveness* to your book — a living relationship between what you're writing and what wants to be written. And this means you're not in it alone.

You can reflect on this for yourself in the following Workbook Reflection, "Re-Trace your Path of Inspiration."

- WORKBOOK -

REFLECTION 3
Re-Trace Your Path of Inspiration

What wisps, whispers, and cloud-traces of inspiration have already suggested themselves to you for your book? (Hint: They might not have come in words, but more as a felt sense, an image, an impression, even a scent.)

The way to make this inner connection is to relax, rather than strain for it. Just think back on what it was like when you realized you wanted to write a book. What told you that? What were the circumstances in which you had that realization? (For example, did you wake in the wee hours with a sense of it? Were you taking a walk in nature? etc.) See if you can return to that experience of receiving the "call," and make it conscious. What called you is an inner presence that will help you throughout the writing of your book.

What wisps, whispers, and cloud-traces of inspiration have already suggested themselves to you for your book?

*{This Reflection practice now comes to a close.
You can continue in a notebook, now or later, if you like.}*

THE BENEFITS OF EVOLVING A TABLE OF CONTENTS

When you evolve a TOC, you get to discover and use much more of yourself than when devising outlines, which are a product of the left-brained analytical mind. Helpful and essential as it is to have your logical mind in good working order, the following caveat from the Sufi mystic Hazrat Inayat Khan is very to the point, here:

> "The mind must be one's obedient servant; when it is a master, life becomes difficult."

When the logical mind takes on the task of the trajectory of your book, its conclusion may make sense on a certain level, but the trajectory may be forced or generic, and the "more" of you is likely to be left out. Although writing an outline is a common practice and formula, why subject yourself to this when you can encounter so much more of yourself by evolving a TOC?

> When you evolve a TOC, you get to discover and use much more of yourself than when devising outlines.

When an Itinerary Isn't Possible (or Even Advisable)

It would probably be easier for the logical, cognitive mind to have a clear outline to follow from the outset — as if your as-yet-unwritten book were a destination and you were simply plotting out an itinerary to get you there ("First we'll take this route, and then we'll take that route, and then we'll connect with this route, and then we'll be there").

But sometimes this isn't always possible. And sometimes it's not even advisable.

If your book is about a topic you already know very well — something you've thought about for quite a while, or talked about it, or even written about on a smaller scale, so that its rough edges have been smoothed out by your going over the intricacies of the subject in your mind over time — then this is a route you've taken already, and your book can largely just retrace your steps. This is a situation where having an outline can potentially be helpful.

But even so, just making point after point in chapter after chapter doesn't automatically breathe *life* into the writing, doesn't enliven you as the *writer* in the act of articulating these points. And if *you* don't feel enlivened while writing, the *reader* isn't likely to feel that, either.

> Just making point after point in chapter after chapter doesn't automatically breathe *life* into the writing, doesn't enliven you as the *writer* in the act of articulating these points. And if *you* don't feel enlivened while writing, the *reader* isn't likely to feel that, either.

Your Book Wants to Come to Life, Not Just Check Off All the Boxes: If your book is meant as an *exploration*, however — if you don't know in advance all that you intend to write — if it's more like a "being there" kind of travel, where you start on the path and see where it takes you; or even if you think you *do* know it all ahead of time, but in the process find that something new has emerged that changes your course from that point on — then delineating an outline at the outset is not really of much use to you. When you're starting your book with a call but not yet a clear destination, then you will need to make use of more than just your logical, cognitive mind — the mind that can do a lot with what it knows but can't see *beyond* what it currently knows.

The "More" of You

You know, somewhere inside you, that there *is* more of you — the "more" that doesn't always get tapped or even invited, in externally dictated writing situations (school, career, etc.), but that can inspire and even heal you in the course of your writing when it is *internally* motivated.

The essential locus of your "more" is your heart. This deeper fount of wisdom and guidance knows things that your cognitive mind can't know all on its own. "The mind is the surface of the heart," said Hazrat Inayat Khan. When the heart is allowed to lead, the mind will help carry out its guidance. The heart can't be *made* to do anything, it can't be *ordered* to produce an inspiration. But you can set up conditions conducive to inspiration that will invite your heart to give you its guidance and its gifts.

> *You know, somewhere inside you, that there is more of you. You can set up conditions conducive to inspiration that will invite your heart to give you its guidance and its gifts.*

Your "more" also includes other aspects that the outline-in, top-down approach fails to call on — for example, your imagination, your feeling nature, your sensing nature, your subconscious, your spiritual/soul connection. All these can come in to help you write a Table of Contents that gradually reveals the organic evolution of your book — and nourishes you in the process.

In this book, you'll learn to let inspirations come to you by their own agency and write them down when they do. Then you can see the larger picture that the pieces are cohering towards. This larger picture will be your completed Table of Contents.

When your cognitive mind is not interfering with or trying to control what's seeking to make itself known to you, but instead takes a back seat to the "more" of you, you'll be able to receive the book that wants to be written as it suggests itself to you in all the organic ways it will.

> *You can learn to let inspirations come to you by their own agency and write them down when they do, then see the larger picture the pieces are forming.*
>
> *When your cognitive mind is not interfering with or trying to control that which wants to be known, but instead takes a back seat to the "more" of you, then you can naturally receive the book that wants to be written as it suggests itself to you in all the ways it will.*

The bits of writing that make their way to you may not show their larger trajectory right away; they may even be a bit puzzling, at this point. You may wonder, "What is *this* about?" "What's the point of *this*? Where is it *going*?" But they are indications, at the very least — perhaps direct clues — perhaps even solid pieces of writing, "keepers," whose context[5] have yet to be known.

By working with this book, you'll find ways to open the door of your inner being to receive the writing that your heart has to give you. You'll learn to invite in those first bits of writing that show the emerging territory — those early pieces that, when viewed together, will cohere enough that you can give each one a "working title"[6] and put onto a page that you title the "Table of Contents," then gradually see how they interrelate and the inclusive picture that forms out of that.

You can reflect on this for yourself in the following Workbook Reflection, "What 'More' of You Hasn't Yet Been Invited into Your Writing?"

~~~~~~~~~~

[5] That is, what is the part, chapter, or subsection that eventually will hold it?

[6] What you call it for the time being. A working title may stay the same, or evolve into a different final form in the course of the book's creation.

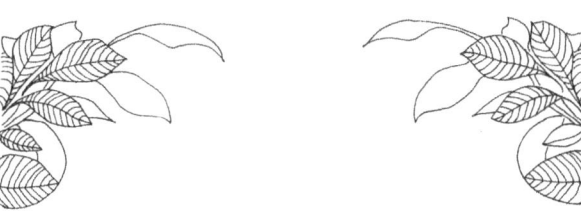

~WORKBOOK~

REFLECTION 4
What "More" of You Hasn't Yet Been Invited into Your Writing?

A major purpose of this book, and of the Writing from the Deeper Self approach in general, is to help you connect *yourself* with your writing. Too often, we have been taught to write *outside of* ourselves so that we don't get to be fully engaged. Or perhaps we have been encouraged to make ourselves the *focus* of our writing, but on a factual rather than contemplative level, so we don't gain deeper insights about ourselves that would also reveal our readers to themselves.

- Reflect back on times when you have written something because you were supposed to. What aspects of yourself did you draw from?

- Was your writing mostly derived from mental thought?
- How much was heart-based?
- What was that like for you?

- Did you write ideas that you'd already had in mind, or did ideas open up *because* you were writing?
- If they opened up in the act of writing, what was that like for you as it happened?
- What did it tell you about what you were capable of?

- If you wrote about yourself, did you write stories or incidents from experience?
- If so, what dimensions of you were involved?
- What was it like for you to do it?
- What was your energy like when you had finished (e.g., enlivened, refreshed, exultant, drained, depleted, discouraged…)?

- To what do you attribute that state of energy in relation to what you wrote and where in yourself you wrote it from?

- Were there unexpected things (topics, understandings, conclusions, for example) that only became conscious for you because you were writing?
- What was that like for you?
- What inner dimensions in you might have been involved or activated by the writing process?

- What "more" of you would you *like* to have come into your experience of writing?

*{This Reflection practice now comes to a close.
You can continue in a notebook, now or later, if you like.}*

Three

HOW TO EVOLVE A TABLE OF CONTENTS

It's as Much About You as About Your Book

CHAPTER THREE

A TABLE OF CONTENTS · HOW TO EVOLVE

NOTE: This chapter offers the following "Reflections" to help you find your way conceptually and concretely:

- *Reflection 5: "Accessing Your Heart's Wisdom through Its Rhythm"*
- *Reflection 6: "Enlist Your Body to Help Evolve Your TOC"*
- *Reflection 7: "Steeping"*
- *Reflection 8: "Incubating a Response During Sleep"*
- *Reflection 9: "Meditating on Your TOC"*
- *Reflection 10: "Praying About What Belongs in Your Book"*
- *Reflection 11: "Integrating Your Glimmers into a More Whole Picture"*
- *Reflection 12: "Giving the Cognitive Mind Its Right Place"*

The real mother lode for evolving a Table of Contents that works both for you as the writer and later on for your readers exists not in a formula outside you, but in making conscious use of capacities that rest *inside* you.

THE INTELLIGENCE(S) INSIDE YOU
(IN ADDITION TO COGNITIVE)

Often, nonfiction writers come away with the impression that their books don't require creativity or feeling (the kind of connection with their material that fiction writers deal in) — that it's enough to get the ideas down clearly and give some examples, even if they never lift off the page and into the readers' capacity for deeper engagement.

This is a very literal definition of nonfiction, and it's based on the convention that the cognitive mind, the prefrontal cortex of the brain, is the only part of the writer that needs to be consulted.

> *The real mother lode for evolving a Table of Contents that works both for you as the writer and later on for your readers exists not in a formula outside you, but in making conscious use of capacities that rest inside you.*

You Contain Many Facets of Intelligence: However, you inherently contain *many* facets of intelligence, not only analytical. So when you get to bring *more* of yourself into the process of determining what will be in your nonfiction book and in what order, not only do you have more modalities to choose from but you also get to enjoy what it's like to experience the play of harmonies inside you instead of applying just a single, one-size-(doesn't)-fit-all note.

> *When you bring more of yourself into the process of determining what will be in your book and in what order, you have more modalities to choose from. You also get to enjoy experiencing the play of harmonies inside you.*

In addition to your analytical intelligence, which compares and contrasts and sees in terms of categories and hierarchies, you also have (at least) these aspects of intelligence:

- *Heart* The heart has its own inclusive way of knowing, and so it sees things (and beneath things) that the analytical mind can't even admit as evidence. When the heart's intelligence is consulted, gifts of feeling and inspiration flower and come close. And it's also through the heart that connections among what may otherwise seem separate and disparate become apparent.

- *Body* The body speaks to us in ways that go beyond the mind's "should I, or shouldn't I?" conflicts, through the language of the felt sense. When we listen to the body, things that we may only have thoughts about become revealed with a sense of certainty and inner knowing.

- *Subconscious* This intelligence isn't concerned with the classifications, departments, and compartments that are the analytical mind's province. Instead, it reaches underneath these mental structures to offer whole new perspectives, often shown to us symbolically or metaphorically. So we come to understand things in surprising, even illuminating ways that the conscious mind couldn't have come up with on its own. And this can be put to the service of evolving a TOC.

- *Spiritual* Innate to our existence, this is often covered over by accrued impressions, experiences, and outer influences, but it is always available right now and right here. That place in us that already *is* in contact with our larger Being is available to us here. This intelligence can be contacted for inspiration, true clarity, perceiving the truth beyond what our ego-mind can see, and much more.

- *Integrative* **Intelligence,** which finds links and connections and unity, and moves towards the *whole* inherent in the parts. While this corresponds to how the right brain works, it's also about the connection between your individualized soul and the larger, behind-it-all universal Presence. So *you* are a part in which the Whole resides; and the integrative intelligence inherent in you seeks ways to connect the apparent parts so that they reveal and reflect this Wholeness. This innate process of connecting can be called on to find a unifying structure for the slowly visible contents of your Table of Contents.

All these Intelligences are in you and open to you, especially when you consciously make room for them.

Given all these intrinsic avenues of Intelligence available in you, you may understand why using only your analytic Intelligence to determine what belongs in your book and in what sequence is like using a garden spade to plant an orchard: a good tool, but so much less than what could better make the large expanse of trees in an orchard bear fruit.

> *Using only your analytic Intelligence to determine what belongs in your book and in what sequence is like using a garden spade to plant an orchard.*

Here are just a few ways you can encourage your non-analytical intelligences to help you grow a Table of Contents organically.

HEART INTELLIGENCE

Rhythm and Heartbeat

The heart is so much the foundation of most *non*-nonfiction writing, why deny yourself the pleasure and dimensionality of its gifts? Just because you're writing a nonfiction book doesn't mean you can't consult your deep and bottomless heart, and mine its treasures to find out what wants to be in your Table of Contents.

The heart is the seat of *feeling*, and of universal wisdom. It's where we know our connection to everything. Clearly, it has a valuable part to play in writing your book. But even in evolving your Table of Contents it can be a great helpmeet, letting you know what's *truly* important to you (not because you've been influenced to think that something *should* be included).

A simple way to get to your heart's gifts is through its rhythm and heartbeat. Breathing in synch with the heart's rhythm can bring you to a more internally connected place inside yourself, and reveal not only what wants to be known but even the *beauty* of what wants to be known through you.

You can reflect on this for yourself in the following Workbook Reflection, "Accessing Your Heart's Wisdom through Its Rhythm."

- WORKBOOK -

REFLECTION 5
Accessing Your Heart's Wisdom through Its Rhythm

The heart beats constantly and automatically, but when you can become aware of its rhythm you can more easily mine its trustworthy treasures, including what may glimmer for your TOC. Try this out:

(1) Place a hand on your heart and direct your attention and breathing there. It may feel foreign to do this at first, but before long you'll become aware of the beating of your heart and its rhythm.

_____ * _____ * _____ * _____ * _____

(2) Now breathe with that rhythm. Let your belly expand as you inhale and contract as you exhale. 1 – 2 – 3 – 4, for example, is a good breathing rhythm. Or maybe you'll find another rhythm that works for you. Feel how your heart rhythm eases you into a more receptive state so that what wants to give itself to you from within, can.

(3) What glimmers come to you in this rhythm? They may be whole sentences, or they may be simply like flashes of light glinting off a butterfly's wing. Whatever they are, welcome them, and write them down:

Later on, you'll learn to develop and integrate the glimmers that stay with you because they are yours to bring forth.

{This Reflection practice now comes to a close. You can continue in a notebook, now or later, if you like.}

BODY INTELLIGENCE

Listening for What's Here

The body is such a repository of feeling and memories, wisdom and care, that you do yourself a real service by including it when cultivating a Table of Contents. If you haven't before consulted your body for its creative input before, this is as good a time as any to begin.

You are central to the book you write —not only what you think, but also what thinks *you* (your embodied experience). So as you open yourself to finding out what wants to be in your evolving TOC, ask yourself: "How *is* this for me? How do I *feel* about this? What's happening in my body? Am I breathing freely, or holding my breath? Does what I just wrote ring true to me? Is there something I'd like to add or change that might bring it closer to home?" Asking yourself questions like these can bring forth responses that increase your confidence and self-trust.

> *You are central to the book you write —not only what you think, but also what thinks you (your embodied experience).*

You can reflect on this for yourself in the following Workbook Reflection, "Enlist Your Body to Help Evolve Your TOC."

~ WORKBOOK ~

REFLECTION 6
Enlist Your Body to Help Evolve Your TOC

If you already have some glimmers for your book ready to be written (or already written), check in with your body to get its feedback. And if you don't have any glimmers at the moment, see what your ever-at-the-ready body has to offer.

The response may or may not come in words; but when you are connected to your body and listening for its message, you may be surprised by the wisdom and clarity that can come. When all of you is involved, there is no stuckness or procrastination. Glimmers come and flow through you into clearer and clearer articulation.

- What does the *top* of your body have to say about what might belong in your book? (Your crown . . . forehead . . . jaw . . . temples . . . back of the head . . . shoulders . . . and so on.)

- What does the *middle* of your body have to say about what might belong in your book? (Your arms . . . hands . . . torso . . . heart . . . and so on.)

- What does your *lower* body have to say about what might belong in your book? (Your belly . . . hips . . . legs . . . knees . . . feet . . . and so on.)

{This Reflection practice now comes to a close. You can continue in a notebook, now or later, if you like.}

So the act of writing becomes not just productive for evolving your TOC, but even a healing experience in the process. The more you come to know and befriend the "more" of you, the more you have available to draw from and appreciate.

SUBCONSCIOUS INTELLIGENCE

Steeping and Sleeping

The focused nondoing of "activities" such as steeping and sleeping can provide a massive assist in bringing to your conscious mind what can only originate from *beyond* the conscious mind. Getting a sense of what belongs in your book can benefit from these refreshing practices.

Steeping

Think in terms of tea. You immerse a teabag or fresh tea leaves in hot water and let it sit there to expand its flavor and scent into the water. When you first pour the water into the teapot, it is clear in color. After the tea has steeped, the water has the color of the tea. It may be green, or gold, or red, depending on what goes into the tea; but it is now of another order. It is *touched by the tea.*

This dynamic can also take place when growing your TOC. It doesn't have to be a matter of forcing yourself to sit down for hours and not get up until the TOC is done. You can instead "steep" an idea that's calling to you — let it rest inside you until it has infused your awareness with something of its nature. So you might do a focused stint on a topic that might be included in your TOC, and then stop and rest, or do something else that's simple, such as wash the dishes. Meanwhile, as in the old tale of "The Shoemaker and the Elves," while your analytical mind is off-line, the "elves" of your other levels of consciousness are putting things together for you. Then, at some point, a metaphorical bell will ring: "Ding! Your TOC is ready to be added to." And you can add in what has steeped and told itself to you.

You can reflect on this for yourself in the following Workbook Reflection, "Steeping."

 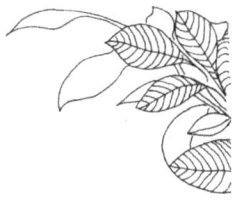

- WORKBOOK -

REFLECTION 7
Steeping

What might you want to steep, in the service of evolving your Table of Contents? Your interest is like the hot water that welcomes the tea leaves to infuse their flavor into the brew. The "tea leaves" are the bits of growing things waiting to unfurl in the hot water. Invite your Steeping Intelligence to give you a hint; or maybe you already know what you want to understand more clearly. It can be something very specific (e.g., "Give me three ways this subject can be spun"), or very broad (e.g., "Give me something about _____ that I can use").

Write down what comes at this early point:

Also note the date and time it came to you:

Date: _____

Time: _____

Now, let it steep. Do something else. Wash the dishes, feed the cat, even tackle your taxes. You do not have to keep what's steeping top-of-mind. When your "tea" has done steeping, it will capture your notice.

When your steeped infusion is ready:

When your questions have steeped and your infusion is ready, it will let you know. Your task is simply to be available for its announcement. Write down what gives itself to you:

What were the circumstances in which it came to you? Were you resting? Taking a walk? Driving the car? Washing the dishes? Working on a different project? And so on.

What does this suggest about the kinds of conditions that are conducive to your steeping?

You might also note the date and time, out of interest in discovering the time interval, in this case, between steeping and receiving the fuller brew.

Date: _____
Time: _____
Time interval between steeping and receiving: _____

{This Reflection practice now comes to a close. You can continue in a notebook, now or later, if you like.}

Sleeping

This is somewhat like steeping, but you don't even need to be as focused or intentional as with steeping. The brain connections and the spiritual inspiration possible during sleep can gift you on awakening with surprising, sometimes delightful inspirations upon awakening, like treasures washed in by the sea onto the shore.

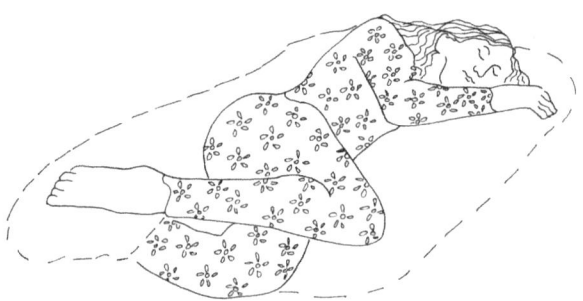

You might receive an understanding of a whole section of your book, or at least a paragraph or two that can lead you further. You might wake with a sense of a certain topic that belongs in your Table of Contents, even though you don't really know what it's about yet. You might get just a glimmer of something, but it clings to you with such dedication that you feel the need to stop everything else for the moment and write it down.

Not only can you make use of your sleeping time to incubate a specific topic, you also can use it to speak to what's so far just a wish or a barely formed question. Then the slept-on reply may spring up when you wake, either as a remembered dream or something that just "appears" in your awake mind. When that happens, grab a pen and paper, or race to your computer, and write it down! Don't let other activities or thoughts get in the way. Slept-on inspirations can be golden.

> *Slept-on inspirations can be golden.*

You can reflect on this for yourself in the following Workbook Reflection, "Incubating a Response During Sleep."

~ WORKBOOK ~

REFLECTION 8
Incubating a Response During Sleep

Before you go to bed at night, place this page of this workbook section close to your bedside, along with a pen. (You can use a notebook just as well.) Write down a question, wish, or even vague desire regarding something that truly fits for your evolving Table of Contents. You are after more than just a word or two. You're asking for deep dream-guidance as to its nature, something you can run with.

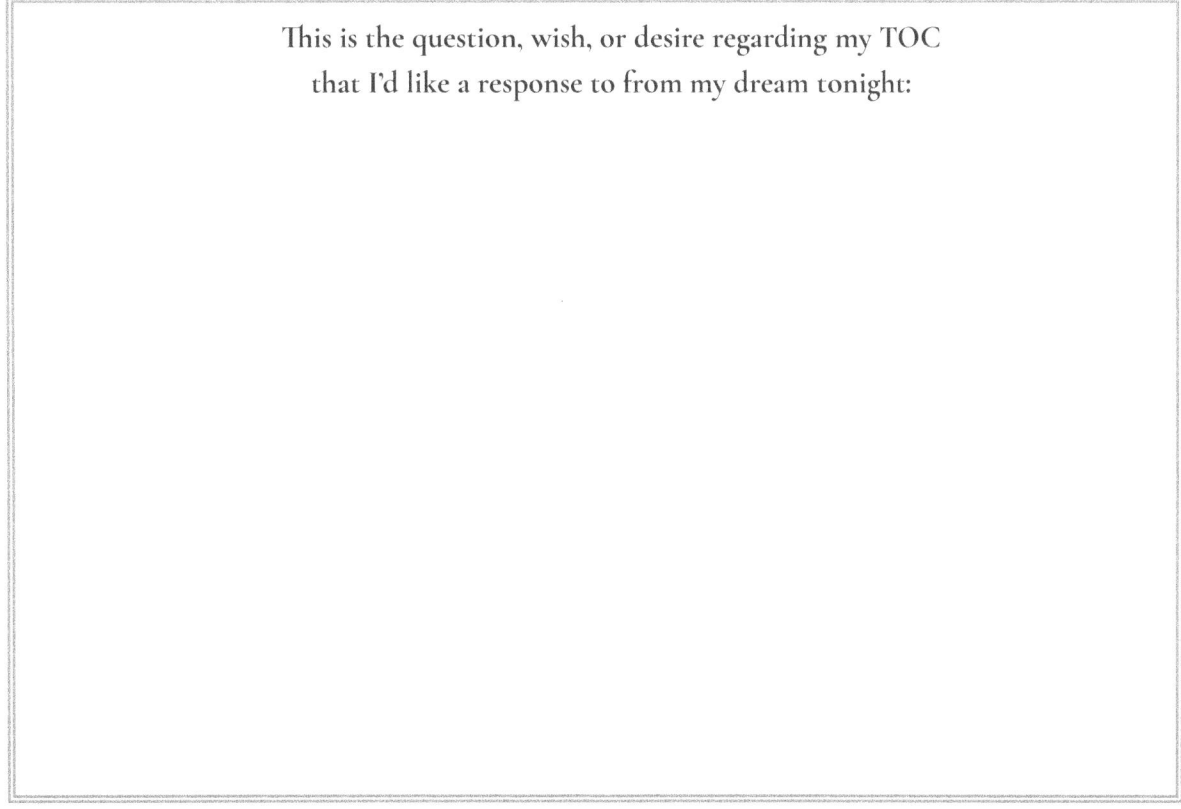

This is the question, wish, or desire regarding my TOC that I'd like a response to from my dream tonight:

Keep this workbook (or a separate notebook) and pen within easy reach from your bed. When you wake up in the morning, write down whatever you remember from your dream.

This is what my dream told me:

Now translate this into writing that you can place in your evolving TOC, in whatever order seems good for now.

(If a good place to put this doesn't readily show itself, later you can bring in your Integrative Intelligence to find a good placement.)

{This Reflection practice now comes to a close. You can continue in a notebook, now or later, if you like.}

SPIRITUAL INTELLIGENCE
Meditating and Praying

Meditating and praying are two complementary ways of contacting your deeper Being, the "you" that's beyond your usual experience of yourself. Meditating involves listening, and praying is a form of speaking (even silently) to the Source from which help can come. So there's listening, and there's speaking — a complete relationship.

Invoking meditation and/or prayer to receive trustworthy guidance on your TOC is not only a good way to find your way with it; it also increases the chances that what comes to you to write will be in line with what you really want in your deeper Being. In the process, meditating and praying can uplift you . . . raise your sights, your reach, and your capacity . . . and connect you with the inner "you" you've longed for. To write from this authentic place is therefore not only functional, but deeply joyful as well.

> *Invoking meditation and/or prayer for guidance on your TOC increases the chances that what comes to you to write will be in line with what you really want in your deeper Being.*

If you already have a practice of meditation and prayer, then it's a simple step to bring the evolution of your Table of Contents into your practice. Just make sure to have a paper and pen nearby so you can write down any glimmers (or fuller directives) that offer themselves to your awareness. They may come right then, in the moment, or later on, in a more "steeped" fashion. So develop the habit of writing them down whenever and wherever they arrive.

> *If you already have a practice of meditation and prayer, then it's a simple step to bring the evolution of your Table of Contents into your practice.*

And if you do *not* already have a familiarity with meditation and prayer, there are a great many ways to make that introduction, if you want to — through books, through talks and practices online, and of course in person in spiritual centers and houses of worship of all denominations. But for the purpose of connecting the nature of your book with your own deeper nature through the gradual discovery of your TOC, here are some ways to enter this rich inner field that you might consider.

Meditation

Though there are many forms of meditation — watching the breath, chanting a sacred name or positive phrase prior to silence, focusing on an image, and so on — the essence of meditation is coming into stillness. Where even though thoughts may (and likely will) come and do the jitterbug while you're sitting there trying to be still, you don't follow those thoughts but instead keep returning to your awareness to the breath, the phrase, or the image. The steadiness of your attention opens you to the still, quiet place inside that is always there under the ego's activity. Whatever glimmers about your TOC you receive from this quieter, deeper site will be trustworthy, arising not from the ego's limiting agenda but from an infinite palette of connection and possibility.

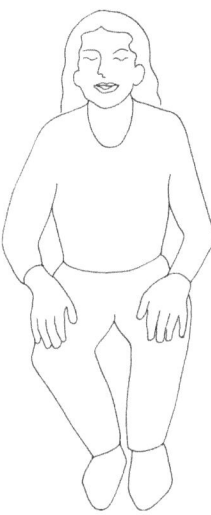

You can reflect on this for yourself in the following Workbook Reflection, "Meditating on Your TOC."

~ WORKBOOK ~

REFLECTION 9
Meditating on Your TOC

Whatever you would like to meditate on is fine. If you're highly visual, you might choose a candle flame, or a flower to look at with open eyes, or you might look at the inside of your eyelids with closed eyes. If you're more auditory, you might close your eyes and listen to the sound of your breathing and/or your heartbeat, or chant a sacred phrase (for example, "Om"). If you're more kinesthetic, you might follow what it feels like as you inhale and exhale — the temperature of the air in your nostrils, or the rise and fall of your belly and diaphragm. Or perhaps it will work best for you to simply follow your breath.

Whatever form your meditation takes, the purpose is to relax the body and the mind, and come to a place of stillness. This inner stillness is a wellspring of inspiration. Achieving total silence might be challenging, but as you get further from the surface of your mind and closer to the depths, you'll find that the *kinds* of thoughts that arise are more inspired.

So try this:

1. Choose a place to be where you won't be interrupted.

2. Place a pen and some paper within arm's reach.

3. Sit down on a firm but comfortable chair or cushion.

4. Close your eyes.

5. Relax as best you can. You might notice if any part of your body or mind is calling out for your attention (e.g., muscle tension, certain thoughts, etc.), and give it attention. (It's amazing how bringing attention to persistent aches and pains can soothe them, like attending to a cranky child.)

6. Now bring your attention to your chosen focus of meditation. Keep your attention there. When it wanders off, bring it back.

7. As you settle into a quieter, deeper inner experience, bring your Table of Contents to mind. Don't force anything, just hold it lightly.

8. See if any glimmers arise as you keep your meditative focus. As they do, slowly reach for the pen and paper, and write down what you received. When the transmission stops, put the paper and pen down and continue with your meditation.

9. The above process (#8) may happen once, or several times. Catching the glimmers as they are given is likely to ensure a clarity and freshness that "trying" to come up with material for your TOC would prevent.

10. When you feel complete, thank yourself for this time of patient sitting, gently open your eyes, look around you with a soft gaze, wiggle your fingers and toes, and get up and re-enter your day (or night). You may feel inspired to write some more, or just let it all come to rest for now.

{This Reflection practice now comes to a close. You can continue in a notebook, now or later, if you like.}

Note: I have recorded an engaging "Meditation for Writers" to help you connect with the creative place within and bring forth what's in you. To request this audio, email me at naomirosedeepwrite@yahoo.com

Prayer

It's easy to suggest ways to meditate, because it's all about getting the extraneous out of the way. But when it comes to suggesting ways to pray, this becomes more difficult, in my view, because prayer is such an intimately personal and private experience. Even when people are praying in a group, if it really works it's still an intensely private experience.

Might some of this be due to the vulnerability that leads us to prayer? We have to admit that we don't know, that we don't "have it all together," that we need help from Someone beyond our immediate self whom we can ask help of, bow to in some form. Even people who don't consider themselves religious sometimes feel drawn to a prayer-like inner stance, whether they follow up on it or not.

> *Prayer is an intimately personal and private experience.*

What, then, has this to do with praying for help with the contents and sequencing of your book? What if you're just a bit puzzled, rather than desperate? What if asking on bended knee is not what you feel called to, and you mostly want clarity of a higher order on your path rather than just another person's opinion?

That's good. It's *all* good. Simply making the contact is good. You may need to have the felt experience that what called you to write a book in the first place will travel with you before and behind you, and won't strand you enroute by the side of the road. It's important to reach out for support and guidance from this Source of Glimmers. Just doing this breaks the confining hold of the frightened separated self, and allows room to receive in the space that this asking makes possible.

> *You may need to have the felt experience that what called you to write a book in the first place will travel with you before and behind you, and won't strand you enroute by the side of the road.*

It's been said, "If you take one step towards God, God will take fifty steps towards you." Praying for guidance on your TOC is taking one step. Then, make room to receive the response from the Divine as the fifty steps on the other end make their way into your world.

You can reflect on this for yourself in the following Workbook Reflection, "Praying About What Belongs in Your Book."

~WORKBOOK~

REFLECTION 10
Praying About What Belongs in Your Book

What can you ask for? Anything as small as the equivalent of a lost button (it's been said, "If you lose a button, ask God for help finding it"). Anything as large as an understanding of the entire book (but it might be overwhelming to receive that all at once).

Why not see where you are with your book right now, and then let your prayer take you one step beyond that?

Where I am with my book right now:

Asking for help via one step beyond:

You can also go all out and ask for *many* steps to be shown, or ask for a *leap* in understanding. This is fine, too. The process of evolving a TOC is fluid until the point where everything feels like it's in its right place, so if a leap of understanding shifts the structure you thought your book should have, tuning to what feels most right will help you redo and refine the rest.

> Where I am with my book right now:
>
>
> Asking for a leap of understanding:

Receiving the responses:

As for the nature of the *response*, keep an open mind. It might indeed come as words, phrases, even paragraphs that you can write down as fast as you can so you capture every last precious drop. But the responses may also come in nonverbal ways — a sense you'll get, an impression resurrected in your memory, a song that pops into your mind. Or they may show up in the outer world and hold significance for you because of your prayer. You might be driving in traffic and find yourself behind a car whose license plate spells out a message that your prayer has tuned you to.

The practice of prayer isn't limited to your life as a book writer. But you can bring it in here, too, and watch as the trust between you and the Larger Guidance develops, and brings your book's structure and nature into view.

> My prayer:

The response:

How I might integrate the response into my TOC:

{This Reflection practice now comes to a close. You can continue in a notebook, now or later, if you like.}

INTEGRATIVE INTELLIGENCE
Glimmer-Gathering

You may find this intelligence coming in later than sooner, once you have written some pieces to be integrated into the bigger picture. But even from the start, you can begin to gather *glimmers* — not-yet-defined, sometimes even hardly visible *senses* of what wants to be part of your book, like catching the wisp of a cloud and pulling it closer so you can see it closer-up. In truth, such glimmers are always available, even if out of the corners of our eyes. When we don't over-focus, their butterfly-like wings create enough light for us to notice them. If we don't dismiss or overlook them, we can gather them in one place (say, a file that we title "Glimmers") and then see how they might come together.

This question, "How might these come together?" is very valuable to keep in mind. First, it will remind you that perhaps seemingly disparate or not-yet-very-formed things *could* conceivably come together. And second, it will ground you in the integrative intelligence itself, so that this innate capacity stretches its muscles and makes you strong in its ways.

Later in this book, you will see the integrative intelligence in action in *my* writing. But you'll learn as much or more by giving it a place in your own inner writing-toolkit at this point.

You can reflect on this for yourself in the following Workbook Reflection, "Integrating Your Glimmers into a More Whole Picture."

~ WORKBOOK ~

REFLECTION 11
Integrating Your Glimmers into a More Whole Picture

Now that you've had the chance to invite some glimmers in and catch others on the wing, you may think you've got just a pile of interesting but unrelated writing. That's probably not the case. The connections may be obvious or they may be subtle, but if you *ask* to see the connections, they will show themselves to you. Once you see them, you may be able to use the pieces of writing as is, or they may need to be restructured and refined as you go.

That's all right. That place in you that has given you the glimmers so far can be counted on to stay with you and guide you all the way throughout the book-writing process. The most important thing is that *you* feel connected.

Go back and look at all the glimmers you have written down so far. Write down what each one seems to be about:

Glimmer 1:

Glimmer 2:

Glimmer 3:

And so on.

Now ask yourself, **"What do these have in common?"** Write down everything that comes without evaluating it at this point:

Once you have a sense of this common thread (whether a "Eureka!" celebrational sense or a more tentative, "I *think* so" sense), let it steep for a while. When the "brew" is ready, it will let you know, and it will feed you more clarity and inspiration.

{This Reflection practice now comes to a close. You can continue in a notebook, now or later, if you like.}

I think you get the picture. You can find and open to other ways of "glimmer-gathering" that call to you. Making the subject conscious will start things moving. That's all you need.

All these other intelligences that are part of your makeup are profoundly important helpmeets in writing your book, and in evolving your TOC.

AND LET'S NOT FORGET ABOUT COGNITIVE INTELLIGENCE
It Has a Role to Fulfill, Too

I've gone into all these other intelligences that are part of your makeup because they tend to be ignored or not made conscious when it comes time to determine what should be in a nonfiction book. I wholeheartedly believe that they are profoundly important helpmeets in writing your book, and in evolving your TOC. And they can be freeing for a great many things you give your attention to — as well as even fun!

Clearly, as I have noted, I don't recommend depending *only* on the cognitive mind to determine the course of your book. Its limitations can dampen, even stifle your creativity . . . lead to generic, template-like solutions . . . and erode your initial motivation to the point where you may be tempted to bail on your book altogether. Yet the cognitive mind does have an important role to play in evolving your Table of Contents.

Your cognitive, analytical mind has an essential function when it comes time to:

- *Name* the writing pieces that you came up with, so you can quickly tell what each piece is about and how it might relate to the other pieces.
- Determine their *logical placement* in your TOC.
- *Suggest topics* you hadn't thought of earlier that could make sense to include.

The cognitive mind is in its element at this juncture: not *creating* the topics that your freer writing has unearthed, but *ordering* them, *sequencing* them, and even determining where *bridges* are needed between one topic and another.

Overall, your cognitive intelligence can support you not by dictating from the top down what you should put into your TOC, but by taking the existing writing pieces that your deeper intelligences have brought forth, and arranging them in a logical progression — one that didn't *initially* develop in that order but that, once viewable on the page, looks as if it had been the plan all along. It's just that it comes in *after* the fact to support what your deeper intelligences have to offer, rather than starting you off by dictating a progression of topics in an abstract, "What will I actually *write* about this?" way.

> *Your cognitive intelligence can support you not by dictating from the top down what you should put into your TOC, but by taking the existing writing pieces that your deeper intelligences have brought forth and arranging them in a logical progression.*

Whether you tend to lead from the top-down or from the bottom-up, there's a place and a timing for your natural way. You can lean into that way, and bring in the other way when it's time. This makes evolving your Table of Contents something that you can work with more intimately — and that helps you discover more of yourself in the process.

You can reflect on this for yourself in the following Workbook Reflection, "Giving the Cognitive Mind Its Right Place in Structuring Your Book."

~ WORKBOOK ~

REFLECTION 12
Giving the Cognitive Mind Its Right Place in Structuring Your Book

"The mind is a good servant but a poor master." — Hazrat Inayat Khan

If the following feels applicable to you —

(1) Recall a situation where your cognitive mind tried to take on the role of "master," in your life— to run the show.

What was the context? Where did the cognitive mind lead your thoughts and efforts? And what was the result?

(This could have taken place in the realm of seeking to create something . . . or make a decision that perhaps the "more" of you needed to be consulted about . . . or something else where you followed your cognitive mind and the results weren't what you really wanted.)

(2) With your current understanding of the role of the cognitive mind in evolving a Table of Contents (and evolving your book as a whole) —

Which of your "more" intelligences (Heart / Body / Subconscious / Spiritual / Integrative) would you have liked to *invite into the process* to lead you where you wanted to go?

```
┌─────────────────────────────────────────────────────────────────┐
│                                                                 │
│                                                                 │
│                                                                 │
│                                                                 │
│                                                                 │
└─────────────────────────────────────────────────────────────────┘
```

(3) How might bringing in a deeper intelligence have brought you closer to the fulfillment of your desire — in terms of the *results*:

THE INTELLIGENCE:	RESULTS FROM BRINGING IN THIS INTELLIGENCE:
Heart:	
Body:	
Subconscious:	
Spiritual:	
Integrative:	

(4) How might bringing in a deeper intelligence have brought you closer to the fulfillment of your desire — in terms of *your relationship to yourself* at the time (and maybe also afterwards):

THE INTELLIGENCE:	HOW I EXPERIENCED MYSELF BY INCLUDING THIS INTELLIGENCE:
Heart:	
Body:	
Subconscious:	
Spiritual:	
Integrative:	

(5) This part is *my* reflection, to illustrate the point that the cognitive mind makes a good servant but a poor master. Before I wrote the actual reflection on "Giving the Cognitive Mind Its Right Place," my cognitive mind barged in and gave me an assignment (an "outline," so to speak) to address the topic "Honoring the Cognitive Mind." That did make sense to me; after all, I'd just before written about the salutary role of the cognitive mind in evolving a Table of Contents.

Dutifully, I wrote down the heading, "Reflection: Honoring the Cognitive Mind," and waited for my cognitive mind to produce something fitting. But nothing came. I could feel a sense of *pushing* in my mind. I pushed a little more; and then I realized the irony of pushing with my cognitive mind in a book about letting things come to you from the Deeper Self and then working with that. So I dropped that focus and instead asked myself, "What's actually arising in my awareness?" Then my deeper Intelligences had the room to help me out.

The reflection that needed to be written, I realized, wasn't about honoring the cognitive mind at all. It was about looking into what happens when you don't honor the *deeper Intelligences*! Once that became clear, the rest followed, and the four steps of this reflection appeared:

(1) Recall a situation.

(2) If you could have included your deeper Intelligences, which would they be?

(3) How could this have encouraged *results* more to your liking than when following the cognitive mind alone?

(4) How could your relationship to yourself have been more to your liking, with the inclusion of the deeper Intelligences?

These organic reflections felt more relatable to me. I could feel into them as I phrased them, so my body, heart, and spirit confirmed that I was on a good track.

And actually, the order in this reflection *did* come from my cognitive intelligence — *after* the fact. I circled back to what I had written and sequenced it after seeing what was in it. Had I set myself the task at the outset of itemizing a series of five, I don't think it would have worked very well — for precisely the reasons this book goes into!

{This Reflection practice now comes to a close. You can continue in a notebook, now or later, if you like.}

Four

AN ILLUSTRATION OF THE PROCESS

Writing Down Your Glimmerings and Seeing the Pattern They Start to Form

CHAPTER FOUR AN ILLUSTRATION OF THE PROCESS

NOTE: This chapter offers the following "Reflection" to help you find your way conceptually and concretely: Reflection 13: "What Have You Learned?"

I hope you have realized by this point that you don't have to have it all together at the outset to begin to realize what belongs in your book. To evolve a Table of Contents that will give you a sense of direction, you just need to:

- Open to some glimmerings (what gives itself to you without your having to push).

- Write them down.

- Reflect on the relationship between one written piece and another (thanks to your Integrative Intelligence).

This will give you at least two valuable things:

- **The beginnings of a Table of Contents.** That is, you won't necessarily situate your beginning glimmer-writings in first place, as Chapter 1, but they will have a place *somewhere* in the TOC. Gradually, as these glimmer-writings accrue, your cognitive mind will enable you to see an *organic order*, and you can position your (titled) pieces in the order that makes most sense to you. (This order can be reworked over time until you feel that it's fully in place.)

- **The experience of unfiltered writing — what it's like to just "let things come."** This is what I've been calling "glimmerings." You let things come *as* they come. This builds a "body of work" and a predisposition to trust yourself, so that when glimmerings give themselves to you, you can say, "Thank you, yes!" and write them down.

As already mentioned, you *will* need to structure your written pieces, with the help of your Cognitive Intelligence (after the fact, or even back-and-forth, like the corpus collosum enabling communication between the left and right sides of the brain). But this way, you will have *living* writings to structure—writing that is as engaging for you to read as it was for you to write.

AN ILLUSTRATION OF THE PROCESS

The procedure is to let pieces of writing come to you, glimmers. I say "*come to you*" on purpose: there's no need to force anything or try to be clever. If you have made yourself available in the ways this book suggests, glimmers of writing *will* come. Your task is to write them down without self-judgment. Later, when you see where they might want to be heading, you'll be glad you let them be. They can always be refined down the road.

> *If you have made yourself available in the ways this book suggests, glimmers of writing will come.*

(1) WRITING DOWN WHAT COMES
Two or More Glimmer-pieces That May Arrive Independently of One Another

Glimmers *will* come, and when you know that you can write them as is, in the moment they come, you can let go of any concerns about "But what do I *do* with this?" or "Where does this *go*?" The first step is to be present to what gives itself to you, and to write it down when it arrives.

To illustrate this process, here are two of my own glimmer-writings that I came up with. I had no agenda for anything specific to happen. I just wanted to be open to what came. When it did, I went with it just as it gave itself to me.

Glimmer #1:

I cannot imagine why people go to the supermarket when they could buy directly from a farm. So many farms now offer direct-to-consumer buying, and for slightly more than the cost of a Safeway receipt you can get zucchinis that still bear traces of the dirt they grew in, chard so tall and leafy that the life-energy still vibrates from its leaves, beets that are large and globular and still attached to their wreath of greens, which also can be cooked deliciously. And so much more: radishes, green beans, tall thin blades of still-growing wheatgrass, oranges, kiwis, mushrooms, on and on.

Every three weeks, a large cardboard box of produce straight from the farm shows up outside our front door. There's always a sense of Christmas-like anticipation (even though I'm the one who placed the order, so I know exactly what to expect). Still, it's a thrill for this city-born and -bred gal to see the fruits and vegetables of the farm waiting for me when I open up the box—the size of the produce, the colors: gold beets, red radishes, green chard so big it has to be folded over to fit in the refrigerator. I love unpacking the box, laying out each remarkable item on the kitchen counter, then putting it away as suggested on the accompanying newsletter (apples on the counter, carrots in the refrigerator bin). Later, I will make some of the chard for supper and some into a health smoothie I can have in the mornings. I will roast the beets and put the greens in a soup. I will roast the radishes, so that their sharp bite turns sweet. And I will read the farmer's note detailing how the farm is doings this season, what's growing, what's fading, the weather, the birds, the bees, what he knows from generations of farming that make his background so very different from my own.

A new box of produce is due tonight. I think there will be corn. It's been ages since I had fresh corn. I remember summers as a child, the sweet burgeoning corn on the cob with butter and salt, and life in the outdoors before any worry about climate change. Bicycles safely in the street, and playing outside until called in for supper. All this simple, natural goodness!

~ ~ ~ ~ ~ ~ ~ ~ ~ ~ ~ ~

Glimmer #2:

I learned to do print-making in my early twenties. I had moved across the country, and my roommate went to an art school. She snuck me in one day, and from that day on I was hooked.

Making linoleum cuts (not the kitchen-floor kind, but the art-supply kind), or "linocuts," was the first project I was introduced to.

I really got into the process: drawing an image on the linoleum block, then cutting away those parts of the linoleum that you didn't want to be visible in the print, then using a brayer to ink the top of the block. Then I would place the inked block on the heavy-duty printing press — a long flatbed, weighted cylindrical rollers, a pressure gauge, and a hand crank. Washing my hands clean so they wouldn't stain the paper, I'd place a sheet of heavy art-paper into a water-filled basin for dampening, then lift it up, blot off the excess water, and carefully lay it on top of the inked block. Then I'd put a few felt pads larger than the block on top of the paper to protect it from the force of the press, and start cranking the roller so it traveled from the top of the flatbed all the way down to the bottom. The muscular strength that was needed, that "Rosie the Riveter" feeling as my upper-arm muscles worked to turn the crank evenly. And then came the main event: peeling the paper off the carved and inked linoleum block to see how the print came out. There was magic in seeing this "proof" plucked from the printing press. First there had been an idea, then a laborious translation onto a thick slab of linoleum, and finally, presto! The moment of unveiling.

I loved everything about this process — seeing it all the way through, the transference of the image in my mind onto the linoleum, and then all the ground-level gruntwork of making it happen. And finally falling in love with the print. Somehow, it had managed — through *me*! — to transfer itself from "just" an idea in the beginning to this utterly real, formed image; unerasable, permanently inked onto good art paper, and proof of my ability to bring a vision to life.

~ ~ ~ ~ ~ ~ ~ ~ ~ ~ ~

You can certainly write more than two glimmer-pieces before looking to see how they might relate to one another, but I wanted to show the process with just two. Because no matter how disparate your glimmer-writings may seem, they all have at least one thing in common: *you*. So there will be *some* commonality, and it will reveal itself if sought.

(2) PUTTING THE PIECES TOGETHER
Looking for the Relationship

As I consider the above two pieces of writing, I make the assumption that there *is* some connection between them, and that this connection can tell me something about what the book might be that's implicit in these pieces.[7]

~ ~ ~ ~ ~ ~ ~ ~

---

[7] I wrote both these pieces just to illustrate the process, here. They aren't actually going to become part of a book, as far as I know.

In some instances, I might simply have an intuitive sense of how they fit together, and what might come out of that on a larger level. But since I don't have much of that sense right now, I start by bringing in my more logical, cognitive mind to help out, now that I have some pieces of writing towork with. So I will start by giving each piece a working title,[8] and then listing the themes that I notice in each piece.

Writing a Working Title:

- For Piece #1: "Farm Box" (or, "The Farm Comes to the City")
- For Piece #2: "Printmaking" (or, "The Thrill of Making Linocuts from Start to Finish")

Looking for the Themes in What You Wrote:

Themes in Piece #1, "The Farm Comes to the City":
1. Living in the city doesn't mean you can't have some of the benefits of a farm.
2. Farm-fresh deliveries are an anticipated delight.
3. The food in the box seems larger, brighter, healthier than when waylaid by supermarkets.
4. It's so much fun to open up what's in the box and feel its energy, see its size and freshness. A happy surprise (even though I'm the one who placed the order).
5. There's a real naturalness to this that makes me think of the better part of childhood—corn on the cob in summers and life outside, safely playing.

Themes in Piece #2, "Printmaking Start to Finish" (the title wanted to shift)
1. I was introduced to printmaking by a friend, so it was a friendly introduction.
2. I fell in love with the entire, intricate process.
3. (I notice that I wrote all about the *process* of making a print, not about the *images* I came up with that ended up in the prints.)
4. There is something about a hands-on, start-to-finish project that deeply called to me.
5. "Something" very real and tangible came out of what was at first "nothing."
6. The steps fascinated me, every part – the drawing, the gouging, the inking, the dampening of the paper, the printing on the flatbed, the "reveal" of the print on the paper.
7. I can still remember with deep appreciation what this experience was like, in detail, many decades later. It really made an "impression" on me. (Aha!)

~ ~ ~ ~ ~ ~ ~ ~ ~

[8] Again, a "working title" is the title you give a piece of writing for now. It may evolve over time, once you have a larger understanding of what's in it and its relation to the larger whole.

(3) HOW THESE THEMES MIGHT INTERRELATE
An Illustrated Evolution of the Table of Contents

The phrase "*Making an impression*" feels resonant. It emerged naturally at the end of my list of themes in #2, and it intrinsically *feels* right. There are many levels of making an impression that could be explored. (I'm not talking about making a good impression on people — though maybe that might fit in?) But making an impression.... Hmmm. I'm going to try this out in a Table of Contents now, leading with "Making an Impression."

TABLE OF CONTENTS
[In progress]

MAKING AN IMPRESSION
[Working Title]

How Experience, Imagination, and _____* Impress Us
and Help Form Our Sense of Self and the World
[Working Subtitle]

Part I
Ways in Which Impressions Are Formed

Chapter 1: Printmaking: The Actual, Physical Making of Impressions

[Note #1: It happens that I think this actually could come in as Chapter 1, as a good way to introduce the topic. This positioning may change as the TOC evolves.]

[Note #2: At first, I called this chapter simply "Printmaking," but then an explanatory subtitle came to mind. Adding "The Actual, Physical Making of Impressions" might at least help me get my footing in evolving the TOC, and maybe it will also turn out to be useful for readers. Time will tell.]

Chapter 2: _____ *[To come]*

Chapter 3: _____ *[To come]*

[Etc.]

Part II
_____ *[To be filled in later]*

Part III
Impressions from the Larger World

Chapter ____: The Farm Comes to the City

[Note #1: I have an intuitive sense that if there were to be, say, three parts, "The Farm Comes to the City" would be in Part III. Putting it in Part II would introduce it too soon. There needs to be some bridge between the chapter on making art prints and this chapter on bringing the fruits of the farm into urban life. So Part III (for now, at least), it is. "Impressions from the Larger World" connotes a widening-out approach, after the very direct experience of making literal impressions through prints. This now welcomes "impressions" as the metaphor it is morphing into.]

[Note #2: Having just written this about "impressions as a metaphor," I can see the possibility of a Part IV, where the impressions that we take in form our sense of identity. Maybe it would be called "Impressions and Identity." Some impressions are beneficial, and some are not. This could be explored — the role and effect of impressions on the mind and even the soul — as well as personal and collective impressions, and the possibility of undoing, removing unwanted impressions (this can't be done with linocuts, but with effort it can be done with etching plates, the engravings burnished out). So, then:]

Part IV

Impressions and Identity

[Note: After writing the above, I just now got an idea of the word needed to fill in the blank space (*) that I'd inserted in the book's subtitle: "Interpretation"!]

How Experience, Imagination, and Interpretation
Impress Us and Help Form Our Sense of Self and the World

[This is how the deeper Intelligences often work. Steeping, in this case—in the short time between writing the book's incomplete subtitle and coming up with the contents of Part IV.]

[End of TOC for now]

This was as far as I got, because I don't think I'm actually going to write a book about impressions. (Though one never knows.) I wanted to take you through a process to see how a Table of Contents can grow out of one's own receptive process, rather than straining from the forehead to get out an outline. You can see there was a back-and-forth relationship between the creative mind and the linear mind, and it began with receiving two pieces that I had no idea where they would go, or how they might come together. And yet they did.

I could never have thought of designing such a thing from my cognitive mind alone. But in following the glimmerings that *came* to me, and following my interest, the rest opened up. (I was actually quite amazed by the level of detail that emerged in my recollection about making linoleum prints. It's been a great many years since I had that experience.)

A LOOK BACK AT THE TOC PROCESS SO FAR

If you'd like to see a more detailed explanation of how the TOC evolved as shown in the above illustration, you can find it in the **Appendix: A Fuller Picture of How My TOC Illustration Evolved**.

But to keep things simple at this point, here are the basic steps involved—the "Cheat Sheet" that I refrained from leading with (because my wish is for you to trust your own glimmers and Intelligences, rather than follow someone else's template from the outset, even mine).

A "Cheat Sheet" on the Basic Steps

Until this point in the book, I've refrained from presenting my organic approach to evolving a Table of Contents as just a "how-to" step-by-step directive, because I think that leaves out too much of what you're capable of when you invite in the "more" of you. But now that we're close to the end of this book, here's a "cheat sheet" of the basic steps that you can use and refer back to:

1. Write stuff. Let glimmers come, and go with them on the page.
2. Then go back into what you've written and give it a heading (e.g., a title).
3. Put that heading into your TOC.

4. Look at how that heading relates to what else is in the TOC. Does it give you ideas about what else might fit with what's there so far, and where? Is some kind of bridge needed to connect one element to another?
5. You're going to go back and forth between the known and the unknown, looking at what you've written organically, and articulating what that section is about with a heading or title. This makes use of both your creative mind (inspiration appears and you follow it — the right-brain/bottom-up path) and your analytical mind (categorizing what you've written and structuring it in a workable order — the left-brain/top-down path).
6. This is not a "one-and-done" process; you'll spiral between writing down the glimmers you receive and determining their placement in the TOC many times in the course of writing your book. But you may find this an actually *pleasurable* The cross-over use of both brains and bringing in more of your Intelligences can be very stimulating, connecting, and even exhilarating!
7. Taking inspiration from a categorized title or heading that you've put down in your TOC can work to stimulate further impressions, recollected experiences, and ideas to come (the left brain inviting the right brain). Likewise, you can be open to receiving impressions, recollections, and ideas (e.g., by steeping and sleeping) and go with them, then back up to see what you've written and what that writing points to that you can categorize as a heading (the right brain inviting the left brain). You might think of the writing that has given itself to you as a room, and the heading as a door to that room.
8. Directionality possibilities — not only Forging Straight Ahead, but also: Backing Up / Circling Round / Spiraling / Taking a Side Street / (and maybe other ways that will occur to you).

Hopefully, this "Cheat Sheet" will jog your memory if and when you need that. *Just don't make this a template to follow slavishly.* Your own deeper Intelligences have much more to give you than that!

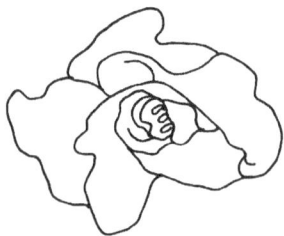

YOUR REFLECTIONS ON THIS EVOLUTIONARY PROCESS

I hope you have been able to follow this process that I've shared with you, and are eager to let its ways inspire your own evolution of a Table of Contents. While the details of my TOC and how they were arrived at may be quite different from how yours will come, your simply hanging in and following the process I just delineated may spark the opening of neural pathways in your brain that will *recognize* this process when it's your turn and your time, and freely give you guidance and inspiration.

Most often, these kinds of steps and leaps and cyclings back, forth, and sideways happen privately, in the creative cocoons of the writers, artists, inventors, and others who give free yet masterful rein to their creative glimmerings. As the reader, you are presented with the finished product and perhaps some behind-the-scenes peeks; but rarely do you get to actually follow the trajectory of a nonlinear approach to something that ends up looking, at the end, as if it had been designed in just that way.

My intention has been to acquaint you with this way, and the Intelligences in you that support it, so that you can have use of a much broader range of yourself from which to evolve the trajectory of your book. By writing it as freely given glimmers as you go, naming what you've come up with, and trying out placements in the TOC until they feel right and settle in, you can relax in the knowledge that not knowing everything ahead of time is really okay, and that the deeper Intelligences in you will guide you true.

In this way, you'll not only evolve a Table of Contents, you'll actually write much of the book along the way.

> *You can relax in the knowledge that not knowing everything ahead of time is really okay, and that the deeper Intelligences in you will guide you true.*

You can reflect on this for yourself in the following Workbook Reflection, "Clarifying What You Have Learned."

~ WORKBOOK ~

REFLECTION 13
Clarifying What You Have Learned

Now that you've come to the end of this book (but not the end of writing your own TOC and book), it would be valuable to conclude this learning experience by reflecting on what you've learned so far.

Of course, as you put it into practice in evolving your own Table of Contents, you'll learn even more from the experience. But for now, you can bring to mind those choice morsels from this book that feel meaningful to you, including those that have introduced you to ways and perspectives you might want to integrate into your own TOC- and book-writing.

The areas you can address here include: The Topic / The Methodology / What speaks to you in that / How you might make use of what speaks to you in your own TOC evolution / Any additional reflections that come to you.

1
TOPIC: Writing Outlines
METHODOLOGY SUGGESTED: Evolving a Table of Contents.

What speaks to me in this / How I might make use of it / Additional reflections:

2
TOPIC: Top-Down vs. Bottom-Up
METHODOLOGY SUGGESTED: Bottom-up can activate deeper Intelligences. Top-down can be brought in later on.

> What speaks to me in this / How I might make use of it / Additional reflections:

3
TOPIC: The Interactive Process
METHODOLOGY SUGGESTED: Use all your Intelligences, let them communicate with each other.

> What speaks to me in this / How I might make use of it / Additional reflections:

4
TOPIC: Models of creating a book
METHODOLOGY SUGGESTED: A "castle in the air"; a statue of clay instead of stone.

> What speaks to me in this / How I might make use of it / Additional reflections:

5
TOPIC: Knowing in advance vs. discovery
METHODOLOGY SUGGESTED: Invite writing-glimmerings to come, then place them.

> What speaks to me in this / How I might make use of it / Additional reflections:

6
TOPIC: The Deeper Intelligences
METHODOLOGY SUGGESTED: Heart / Body / Subconscious / Spiritual / Integrative —
Which are already known to me? Which would I like to cultivate?

> What speaks to me in this / How I might make use of it / Additional reflections:

7
TOPIC: What have I learned about myself in going through this book?
METHODOLOGY SUGGESTED: What you learn about yourself
infuses the book you will be writing.

> What speaks to me in this / How I might make use of it / Additional reflections:

8
TOPIC: What am I inspired to try out?
METHODOLOGY SUGGESTED: Glance back over what's in this book from the beginning and see what stands out that interests you to try out and/or continue.
You also can do this in terms of your own responses to Reflections 1 – 12.

> What speaks to me in this / How I might make use of it / Additional reflections:

9
TOPIC: Any new ideas or attractions — or questions?
METHODOLOGY SUGGESTED: Be present to yourself in this moment, and see if anything comes to you that's new and engaging.

> What speaks to me in this / How I might make use of it / Additional reflections:

AN ORGANIC APPROACH TO STRUCTURING YOUR BOOK ~ 91

10
TOPIC: What glimmerings might be in my book's near future?
METHODOLOGY SUGGESTED: Take a walk ... wash the dishes ...
let your mind go on "repose."
Meanwhile, let things steep. Then see what invites your attention.

What speaks to me in this / How I might make use of it / Additional reflections:

{This Reflection practice now comes to a close. You can continue in a notebook, now or later, if you like.}

A BLESSING ON YOUR WAY AS YOU WRITE YOUR BOOK

Thank you for giving yourself to what's in this book and the ideas, suggestions, and reflections that it offers. I trust you have gained some understanding of how your unique constellation can be put to use, *without alteration*, to evolve a Table of Contents for your book as you go. Now you can be your own teacher!

I recommend that you read this book more than once, with a pen or pencil and a notebook by your side. The purpose of the pen or pencil (much as I myself love writing on a keyboard) is to link you to your heart more directly: when you write with your hand, the movement alone can activate the heart's wise input. Also, you can draw arrows and doodles, and other right-brain expressions that can lead you to a more immediate, less regimented understanding of the subject at hand. And the purpose of the notebook (or journal) is to give you a more spacious place to record your glimmers, questions, responses, and written expressions than the small (but meaningful) boxes provided in this book.

It really *is* a big deal to write a book, especially in a way that speaks to *you* as well as your readers. Too many books these days, especially nonfiction books, are put together with a cookie cutter, and leave the heart and soul (and bodily, subconscious, spiritual, and integrative Intelligences) out of the writing. You, however, now have the opportunity to bring the "more" of you into discovering and writing your book. And evolving a Table of Contents as you go, rather than imposing an outline and trying to fill it in from the top-down, will support you to do this.

May you write the book(s) of your heart by seeing what wants to evolve — and may your faith, confidence, and enthusiasm increase in the process!

(And if you'd like my support beyond what you've gotten from this book, that can be arranged. See the "Next Steps" section, right after the Appendix.)

Blessings on your journey and book-writing!

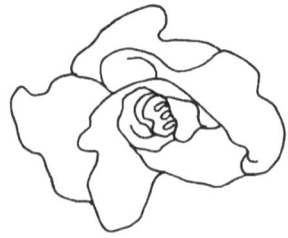

Naomi Rose
Book Developer & Creative Midwife
Creator, Writing from the Deeper Self / www.naomirose.net
Publisher, Rose Press: Books to Bring You Home to Yourself /www.rosepress.com

APPENDIX

A FULLER PICTURE OF HOW MY TOC ILLUSTRATION EVOLVED

This is the same material as the illustration in Chapter Four showing how I used the two glimmer-pieces I wrote to start evolving a Table of Contents. However, this Appendix reveals the original, unedited version — the fuller picture — in case understanding the evolution of my creative process more thoroughly can shed light on what *your* process of evolving a TOC might look something like.

Backing up to reflect on this first-draft TOC, you can see that what I constructed here was not a very linear process. These are the (bottom-up) aspects that were involved. (An outline would have gone in the other direction.)

1. Writing what came to me (two pieces, though there could have been more), without any interference from my logical mind. (#1, below)
2. Assigning each written piece a working title. (Logical mind enters.) (#2)
3. Making a list of themes in each piece. (Logical mind enters.) (#3)
4. Noting what spoke to me in the list of themes (Intuition came back in.) (#4)
5. Drafting a Table of Contents with the information I currently had. At this stage, a structure began to slowly come into visibility — not so much in a linear way as in a connective, associative way. (#5)

    ◦ A subtitle began to emerge
    ◦ I blocked in some Parts (starting with Part I, still untitled)
    ◦ I sensed what would be in Chapter 1 and put that in

- I sensed a subtitle and put that in (note that all this begins to make the TOC evolution feel more *real*, in large part because it's not theoretical but is largely based on the glimmers that came to me)
- I sensed a title for Part I and put it in
- I had nothing yet for Part II, but did receive a title for Part III
- This opened up the existence of a Part IV, and its title
- This opened up the book's full subtitle
- And I now had a draft of the TOC to work with further, one that truly interested me and didn't have to be forced.

Here are the details:

(1)
Writing the Glimmers That Came

I began with no fixed idea in mind, just a receptivity to whatever "glimmers" might come. When they did (whether as an idea, an image, or a phrase), I wrote whatever came and then continued exploring in writing. I wrote *two* pieces (there could have been others as well) so that I could soon see the correlation(s) between them, and so not force a direction from a single piece of writing.

(2)
Assigning a Working Title

I assigned a working title to each piece — #1: "Farm Box" (or, "The Farm Comes to the City"), and #2: "Printmaking" (or, "The Thrill of Making Linocuts from Start to Finish").

(3)
Making a List of Themes

I wrote down the themes I found in each of these two pieces. Though the shortened version in Chapter Four has most of them, here is the *full* list of themes in each piece of writing:

Full List of Themes in Piece #1, "The Farm Comes to the City":

1. Living in the city doesn't mean you can't have some of the benefits of a farm.
2. Farm-fresh deliveries are an anticipated delight.
3. The food in the box seems larger, brighter, healthier than when waylaid by supermarkets.
4. The transaction feels more intimate than in a supermarket, with the cellophane packaging and the time delay between picking and eating.
5. It's so much fun to open up what's in the box and feel its energy, see its size and freshness. A happy surprise (even though I'm the one who placed the order).
6. I feel a connection to the farmer, who includes a newsletter that talks about what's happening on the farm so I can see and feel it in my imagination.

7. The newsletter also instructs me on the storage and cooking of a given vegetable or fruit. If I haven't ordered that one this time, I'll remember it for later on, if I do another time.
8. There's a real naturalness to this that makes me think of the better part of childhood—corn on the cob in summers and life outside, safely playing.

<u>Full List of Themes in Piece #2, "Printmaking Start to Finish"</u> *(the title wanted to shift)*

1. I was introduced to printmaking when I was in my twenties by a friend, so it was a friendly introduction.
2. I fell in love with the entire, intricate process.
3. I had to learn to use sharp tools carefully.
4. (I notice that I wrote all about the *process* of making a print, not about the *images* I came up with that ended up in the prints.)
5. There is something about a hands-on, start-to-finish project that deeply called to me.
6. This had been something unknown to me and out of my reach, and then I was "inducted" into its ways and (to some extent) mysteries.
7. "Something" very real and tangible came out of what was at first "nothing."
8. It was very different making a print than just doing a drawing on paper. It was much more intricate and laborious.
9. The steps fascinated me, every part – the drawing, the gouging, the inking, the dampening of the paper, the printing on the flatbed, the "reveal" of the print on the paper.
10. I felt in a tradition of working with my hands to produce something attractive. "Rosie the Riveter" came to mind (though this was all elective work, nothing of a survival nature — i.e., "rivets" — was being built).
11. I can still remember with deep appreciation what this experience was like, in detail, many decades later. It really made an "impression" on me. (Aha!)

(4)
Noting What Spoke to Me in the List of Themes

At the end of the list of themes that showed up in Piece #2, a phrase came to mind —"Making an impression" — that, itself, made an impression on me. The phrase, and the latent idea behind it, felt resonant and full of potential. I wondered if that might be a theme that could house the entire book. So:

(5)
Doing a Beginning Draft (Sketch) of a Table of Contents Based on This Information and Paying Attention to What Was Emerging

I set up a separate page, which I called "Table of Contents," and tried out "Making an Impression" as the title of the book. This began to make it look more real. And here's where the creative evolution process started to become more visible:

[√] Once I had a title, a subtitle began to form. I wrote down what came, and it felt like there might be *three* elements to include, but I only was aware of two, so I put in a blank line to indicate that there might later be a third: "How Experience, Imagination, and _____ * Impress Us and Help Form Our Sense of Self and the World"

[√] Blocking in some Parts. Then I wrote down "Part I," "Part II," and "Part III," because I know from long experience that the structure of having sections, or "Parts," to contain individual chapters is a helpful one for nonfiction books. I didn't yet know what would fit into them, but I put them in to make the containers. I knew that I did already have two pieces of writing that I wanted to place, "Printmaking Start to Finish" and "The Farm Comes to the City." So I inserted the designation for the three parts (not yet knowing their titles—i.e., focus):

Part I: _____
Part II: _____
Part III: ____

[√] Sensing the presence of Chapter 1. Once I saw "Part I" on the TOC page, I knew that "Chapter 1" would follow, so I wrote that down. As soon as I did, I realized that what I had written on "Printmaking" (Piece #1) could start the book off as Chapter 1, because it provides a literal example of making an impression. So I wrote down:

Chapter 1: <u>Printmaking</u>

[√] Sensing a subtitle. Once I saw the chapter number and title, a subtitle came to my mind. (I really love subtitles; they give valuable context.) So I wrote down:

Chapter 1: Printmaking: <u>The Actual, Physical Making of Impressions</u>

[√] Sensing a title for Part I. Now that I had written the subtitle for Chapter 1, a title for Part I came to me, enabling me to fill in the blank I'd left as a placeholder. Such connections almost *can't* take place in chronological order without straining the cognitive mind; but if you can stay tuned for when they arise naturally, and then insert them where they belong *to the best of your current knowledge*, you may begin to see a solid framework emerge. So I returned to Part I and inserted this title:

Part I: <u>Ways in Which Impressions Are Formed</u>

That made sense, didn't it? If the first chapter (based on Piece #1) was literally about printing impressions, and the other chapter (based on Piece #2) was about another kind of impression, then what did the first level of understanding about impressions (i.e., the title of Part I) need to be, as suggested by the two chapter titles I'd come up with? "Ways in Which Impressions Are Formed" arose to fill the bill.

[√] Checking to see if I had anything to put into "Part II." Then I went on to Part II. I didn't yet have anything in mind for this part, so I skipped it for now and moved on to Part III.

[√] Checking to see if I had anything to put into Part III. As I considered the as-yet-unnamed Part III, intuitively it seemed to me that the piece I'd written on "The Farm Comes to the City" could fit there. So I put it in under Part III. I didn't yet know what the chapter number would be because I had no idea how many chapters would come in between Chapter 1 and this one, so I indicated a "Chapter" but left the number blank.

Chapter ___: The Farm Comes to the City

[√] Looking for the connection between Part I and Part III. Once I saw that the chapter on The Farm Comes to the City" was in the last section that I'd come up with so far (Part III), something in the background of my mind began to play with the question, "What's the connection between what's in Part I and what's in Part III?"

I looked at the difference between literal impressions (Chapter 1, "Printmaking") and more metaphorical impressions ("The Farm Comes to the City"). And I realized that Part III could be about this widening of impressions beyond our own framework of experience. So I gave it a working title:

Part III: Impressions from the Larger World

[√] Sensing something wanting to come into visibility. In working out my "impressions" about "Impressions from the Larger World," I came to realize a potential next part:

Part IV: Impressions and Identity

I found this exciting, because I'm *really* interested in the topic of how the impressions we take in over the course of a lifetime lead us to have a certain view of who we are. I could happily write a book about this subject alone—not because I know everything about it, but because I'm so *interested* in finding out more.

[√] The emergence of the full subtitle. And now that this part had come into visibility — thanks to my most recent understanding (the existence of Part IV) and my steeping-mind — suddenly the word missing from the subtitle of the book flashed into my awareness: *Interpretation*. Yes, that felt right!

How Experience, Imagination, and <u>Interpretation</u>
Impress Us and Help Form Our Sense of Self and the World

> I could have gone on, but I stopped at that point. Sometimes, the mind just needs a rest so it can integrate all that's happened and then come up with more, later.

And that's the full picture of the fuller picture.

I hope you have a feeling for this evolving-a-TOC process, enough so that you can start evolving your own. The process itself will teach you much about how it works. And if you want more guidance than this, see the "Next Steps" section, next.

NEXT STEPS . . .

Good Work! Good for you that you've gone through this book as you have. What you've already received will help you put the structure of your book together. And perhaps it will also help you actually write your book in an organic and resonant way.

But if you find that it could be helpful for you to have more custom-fitted guidance, I'm happy to help. This is what I do as a Book Developer & Creative Midwife.

The book that has called you to write it this far has a heartbeat that's yours. It needs to have your imprint on it, be animated by your soul and your breath.

This is not something you can learn in a weekend, or have an AI do. Your authentic voice — not only what you write, but how it gives itself to you to write it, and from how deeply within — is your holy gift to the Source, to yourself, and to the world. So you really want to listen to what's inside you.

This can be challenging. We have so many external influences crowding our own knowing — whether from family and childhood authority figures, or from the popular view of how we "should" write a book — that our own internal voice can easily be eclipsed. And yet that voice is there. As is a particular way to attend to it, a unique creative pathway that is natural to you.

As the creator of Writing from the Deeper Self (a call that came to me many years ago, well before I understood what it meant), I know that each one of us has it in us to bring a unique and beautiful healing gift to the world, based on our true nature. And that the world is poorer without it, and infinitely richer with it. This gift can take a great many forms. In my professional work, it takes the form of the book of your heart.

TO RECEIVE MY FURTHER SUPPORT:

If you would like my further support for evolving your book's Table of Contents — or for writing your book in full — here are some simple things you can do:

1. Join my mailing list. You'll receive my newsletters as well as information on other kinds of support you might like to have to encourage your creative flowering.
   < You can sign up on my website: https://www.naomirose.net
   < Or you can email me at: naomirosedeepwrite@yahoo.com and put "Sign me up for your mailing list" in the subject line.

2. Sign up for my "FAQ" list for readers of *An Organic Approach*. That way, you'll be alerted when I host an online FAQ session about evolving your TOC.

< To sign up, email me at: naomirosedeepwrite@yahoo.com and put "Organic Approach FAQ list" in the subject line.

3. Request my "Meditation for Writers" audio recording to help you connect to your inner knowing and expression with confidence and trust

< Email me at: naomirosedeepwrite@yahoo.com and put "Meditation for Writers" in the subject line.

4. Book a complimentary 30-minute consultation with me to explore your book-writing dream. If we're a good fit, we'll take our work together further. If not, there's no obligation to continue. (And you may walk away with some valuable insights about your book and creative process that you can use on your own.)

< Email me at: naomirosedeepwrite@yahoo.com and put "Complimentary 30-minute session" in the subject line.

The book that's calling you deserves to be written in a way that honors your own creative nature, and illuminates your knowing of yourself as well as your subject. So you heal in writing the book, and your readers heal in reading it.

I look forward to hearing from you and encouraging your own creative flowering.

Naomi Rose
Book Developer & Creative Midwife
Helping you listen forth the book of your heart.
www.naomirose.net

ABOUT NAOMI ROSE

Perhaps the first thing to share about Naomi Rose is that she writes without outlines and evolves her Table of Contents, just as this book recommends. Her many years in the book industry, especially as an editor, have taught her how to use headings, chapter structuring, and so on to provide a logical developmental sequence after the fact. But she didn't start out knowing how to do this.

Naomi was born into a family of writers and artists, so she picked up certain understandings about writing and creativity by osmosis at an early age. She was drawn to visual art (not a top-down, linear approach at all) from childhood, and in her teens she attended the prestigious High School of Music & Art in New York City. Later, in college and graduate school (a BA from the City College of New York, then an MA from the University of Connecticut), she majored in literature—which, like visual art, was more right-brained than linear. However, the outline-based approach to writing papers that she was trained in promoted an exclusively linear approach. Just because she became good at it didn't mean that she felt truly seen through her writing—either by her teachers, or by herself. A great loneliness ensued from this gap between who she really was inside, and what she was trained to put forth in her writing.

She became an editor in her early twenties, not so much as a career decision but because by that time she knew that the abstruse academic life was not for her. She stayed with this path for decades, working for publishers, businesses, nonprofits, and authors, specializing mostly in nonfiction books. She also wrote and published articles, worked as a consultant, and even illustrated a few books.

Over time, her skills increased exponentially and were helpful in making her clients' books read well. But she became disenchanted with the formulaic approach to writing nonfiction books that was the industry standard. She wanted something more real than the projects she was getting to work on and readers were getting to read. Intuitively, she knew that nonfiction books could go beyond merely providing information and opinions, and be a true mirror of the self—could provide the healing transmission that readers secretly longed for.

Gradually, she combined her editorial experience, her subsequent studies in transpersonal psychology, and her dedicated spiritual path to evolve an approach to writing that she called "Writing from the Deeper Self." This was designed to address the inadequacies of authenticity that she had observed in the industry, and to help authors get closer to themselves through the writing process. She was convinced that both the writer and the writing would benefit, and that readers would inevitably receive the benefits too.

Today, in Naomi's work as a Book Developer & Creative Midwife, she gets to use her heart, her mind, and her professional book experience to help people, including first-time authors, bring their whole selves to writing books. Many books have been birthed into print from this Writing from the Deeper Self vision. She offers complimentary exploratory consultations to those who find her approach of interest, and she can be emailed about this at naomirosedeepwrite@yahoo.com. To get a good sense of her work beyond what's in this book, see her website, www.naomirose.net

In addition, Naomi is an artist. Her illustrations decorate this book. Her series of drawings "Postures of Love" can be viewed at https://www.rosepress.com/postures-of-love-art-prints

Naomi is also the publisher of Rose Press (www.rosepress.com), and the author of the following books on the creative process (in addition to *An Organic Approach to Structuring Your Book*):

[√] *STARTING YOUR BOOK: A Guide to Navigating the Blank Page by Attending to What's Inside You.* (2011)

[√] *GROWING YOUR BOOK by Listening to What's Inside You: A Writing from the Deeper Self Approach.* Coming soon. To be notified when this book is in print, or to pre-order, email Naomi at rosepressbooks@yahoo.com)

ROSE PRESS: A PUBLISHING HOUSE FOR YOUR INNER GARDEN

BOOKS TO BRING YOU HOME TO YOURSELF
~ A publishing house for your inner garden ~
www.rosepress.com

In our time of reading for information, Rose Press seeks to offer you books and other fragrant offerings that will live in your heart like an eternal time capsule, releasing their healing medicine as you need it.

"Fragrance" is not usually associated with books. Books, we tend to think, in our speeded-up age, are about ideas, entertainment, steps for helping us to be more new and improved.

And yet there have been books that are mirrors to the soul—or marvels of excavation, revealing the vast treasures hidden within. There have been books, the journey of whose reading swept readers up into their remarkable world, leaving them at the end with the passage of that journey in their bones, and the fragrance of that atmosphere still hovering invisibly near. There have been books so deeply entered into by their authors that turning the pages of these books transmitted to their readers more than a whiff of the understandings and evocations embodied in the book: they helped to form the readers' very being.

This is the vision of Rose Press books: that in taking them into yourself, you discover what is truly in you, and it opens your heart like petals opening to the light.

That said, getting to the more subtle fragrance—the distillation of more earthbound, sometimes sludgy experience—is often what book writers dream of and work in the trenches to do. Behind the most exquisite fragrance left with a reader by a book is the author's composted experience (all the years and memories and ideas and possibilities dreamed of and lived through, written and refined) that produced such perfume. So what is left on the page is the offering: the "fragrance," one might say. All the dregs have been churned up and left to sink to the bottom, leaving only the gift of the book.

This, then, is what the reader gets to experience: a hint of the churning process, but ultimately, the fragrance.

> *When 10,000 rose petals are gathered in the dark of early morning, placed into retorts filled with solvent, and heated over time until their oil rises as a liquid distillation, then you have just 16 ounces of that most prized (and expensive) of aromatics, rose essence (rose absolute).*
>
> *In the same way, Rose Press Books are the distillation of their authors' essence, distilled over time and many revisions to bring you into contact with the gift of something fragrant and indescribably beautiful within yourself.*

Writing these books entails a journey, and reading these books is also a journey. And you, afterwards, will be the carrier of that journey in the world: burnished, more yourself than before, and smelling — even after everything — like a rose.

OTHER BOOKS & ART BY NAOMI ROSE

Additional books and art by Naomi Rose
are available on the Rose Press website:
www.rosepress.com

BOOKS

From the "Creative Process" Series:

- *Starting Your Book: A Guide to Navigating the Blank Page by Attending to What's Inside You*

- *An Organic Approach to Structuring Your Book: A Right-Brained Alternative to Outlines (Workbook Included)*

- *Growing Your Book by Listening to What's Inside You: A Writing from the Deeper Self Approach.* **Coming soon!** To be notified of publication or to pre-order, email rosepressbooks@yahoo.com

From the "Money and the Inner Life" Series:

- *MotherWealth: The Feminine Path to Money*

- *The Portable Blessings Ledger: A Way to Keep Track of Your Finances and Bring Meaning & Heart to Your Dealings with Money*

ART

"Postures of Love" – prints and commissions. https://www.rosepress.com/postures-of-love-art-prints

www.ingramcontent.com/pod-product-compliance
Lightning Source LLC
Chambersburg PA
CBHW040751020526
44118CB00042B/2856